Improving Student Learning in the Doctrinal Law School Classroom

Improving
Student Learning in the
Doctrinal Law School
Classroom

Skills and Assessment

Kim O'Leary

Jeanette Buttrey

Joni Larson

CAROLINA ACADEMIC PRESS

Durham, North Carolina

Library of Congress Cataloging-in-Publication Data

Names: O'Leary, Kimberly E., author. | Buttrey, Jeanette, author. | Larson, Joni, author.
Title: Improving student learning in the doctrinal law school classroom : skills and assessment / by Kimberly E. O'Leary, Jeanette Buttrey, Joni Larson.
Description: Durham, North Carolina : Carolina Academic Press, LLC, [2020]
Identifiers: LCCN 2020027563 (print) | LCCN 2020027564 (ebook) | ISBN 9781531019358 (paperback) | ISBN 9781531019365 (ebook)
Subjects: LCSH: Law--Study and teaching—United States—Evaluation. | Law schools—United States. | Learning—Evaluation.
Classification: LCC KF272 .O44 2020 (print) | LCC KF272 (ebook) | DDC 340.071/173—dc23
LC record available at https://lccn.loc.gov/2020027563
LC ebook record available at https://lccn.loc.gov/2020027564

CAROLINA ACADEMIC PRESS
700 Kent Street
Durham, North Carolina 27701
Telephone (919) 489-7486
Fax (919) 493-5668
www.cap-press.com

Printed in the United States of America

Contents

Acknowledgments

While this book was being finalized, the COVID-19 pandemic changed the face of legal education almost overnight. Schools across the world were forced into emergency "online" teaching. Some schools continued in an all-online mode, while others developed partial, or "flex" models, combining online and face-to-face instruction. Amidst these chaotic circumstances, many professors are seizing the moment to redesign their courses. Realizing that these new forms of instruction cannot simply replicate what they have been doing in the classroom, these professors are looking for tools to re-imagine their courses. Some of these new tools are purely digital. But other tools—tools such as this book—can help you structure your course design in ways that can improve student learning. Never has there been a more important time to challenge our venerable assumptions about teaching and learning. We hope this book helps.

The authors wish to thank those who have supported and helped us along this journey.

JRB: I thank my husband, Jim, for all his support, encouragement, and running gags. Best play I ever made.

JL: Many thanks to my students who taught me so much over the years.

KEO: Thanks to my spouse, Paul Blaha, for listening to my ideas about teaching for over thirty years, even though he is neither a teacher nor a lawyer, and for always challenging me. Thanks also to Christine Church, Marla Mitchell-Cichon, Vickie Eggers, and my co-authors for teaching me about teaching. As Marla always says, "The only question that matters, when you are an educator, is 'Will this help the student learn?'"

Improving
Student Learning in the
Doctrinal Law School
Classroom

Introduction

Shifting from "Did I teach X?" to "Did they learn X?"

Legal education has created silos where certain professors teach "skills" courses and others teach "doctrine." This book challenges that underlying premise. The three authors of this book are or have recently been law professors who teach legal doctrine by explicitly helping students build the skills they need to understand and apply that doctrine. In our experience, students cannot learn doctrine without explicit instruction in skills. Many law schools offer isolated instruction in first-year skill building; while we applaud that form of instruction, our premise is that skill-building and doctrine should be taught together.

This book offers ideas for how to improve student learning of law school doctrinal courses. Most law professors are busy and find it hard to make the time to alter teaching methods. We have made this book intentionally short and easy to read—without citations, for the most part—so that busy professors can pick it up and find ideas for their courses. We have included workbook pages for each chapter to help busy professors plan activities for their courses. We hope this book becomes something you "do," not something you just read.

First, some definitions. By "doctrinal" courses, we mean law courses whose primary outcome is the learning of a body of legal doctrine, or law. Such courses typically identify by the subject matter, e.g., Torts, Contracts, Property, Tax, Criminal Law, Civil Procedure, Evidence, etc. The skills we address are the general lawyering skills students must possess to understand and apply that doctrine: legal analysis, reasoning, careful reading of cases and statutes, and so on. This is *not* a text about how to teach specific lawyering skills such as client interviewing, client counseling, negotiation, research and writing, mediation, or trial skills. But, it *is* a call to more explicitly connect all lawyer tasks to the doctrinal classroom.

This book advocates shifting our focus as teachers from "Did I teach X?" to "Did they learn X?" Another premise of the book is that it is possible, in fact fairly easy, to know what your students are and are not understanding throughout the course. In each chapter, we suggest how you can easily assess student learning. Assessment can take many forms, and only some of these forms are tests. Discussion threads, group activities, and applied-learning assignments are a few ways professors can assess student learning in non-test settings. The simplest way to know what your students are not understanding is to ask them, something we regularly do.

This text advocates a wide variety of teaching techniques both inside and outside the law school classroom. Recognizing that different students learn differently, it suggests that law professors regularly incorporate active-learning methods to supplement Socratic and lecture methods. Many of the methods discussed in this book can be set up in digital learning management systems.

Finally, a word about "coverage." The most common misperception among law professors is that active learning, frequent assessments, and intentional skill-building reduces the coverage of substantive law. That is a misperception for at least three reasons. First, any given course is limited in how deeply a topic is covered. Coverage is, in some sense, arbitrary. For example, a first-year Property course might "cover" landlord-tenant law in three weeks, but that is not sufficient for any lawyer to understand landlord-tenant law enough to practice in the field. Book authors and professors make judgments about which concepts are core, and about how much detail to cover. Coverage is affected by topics tested on the bar and, to some extent, modern approaches to a field. But no professor can cover everything.

Second, each of us has taught core doctrinal courses and covered exactly the same material, using the same text, as colleagues of ours who just lecture or only use Socratic teaching methods. Active learning techniques and assessment are just different ways to teach the same material.

Third, educational research tells us that these techniques improve student learning. So more coverage of topics, if students are not learning the material, is a waste of time. We also note that digital learning management systems offer a wealth of opportunities to help students structure their learning *outside* of class. While it takes some time and patience to set up these materials, once they are established, many of these tools manage themselves with little additional professor time. Students are amazingly adept at managing digital systems; furthermore, student teaching assistants can help manage digital course management tools, which means that the professor does not have to be solely responsible for maintaining these materials.

We hope that you find our ideas helpful in shifting the focus from what we are teaching to what our students are learning.

Chapter 1

Understanding the Basics of Learning Theory: What You Need to Know

There is an entire body of research and knowledge about best methods for teaching. Leaving aside the ways in which teaching law might be different from other areas of education, what is the same is that students are expected to learn a body of knowledge. Then they are expected to use that knowledge to provide services to others. In that sense, law students are similar to medical students who will practice medicine, or MBA students who will run a business, or a myriad of other students. Building on that commonality, learning theories applicable to medical and business students can inform relevant learning theories applicable to law students.

A. Backward Design Theory: Working from the Desired Result

In backward design theory, professors focus on the desired results (or outcomes) of the course and work back from there. They do this by:

1. Deciding what students should be able to understand and do when the course is over.
2. Determining what evidence professors will examine to establish whether students achieved that goal.
3. Working backward from the goal and intentionally planning the course so that students can reach the desired outcomes.

In other words, all professors should begin the course with a clear idea of where they intend students to end up. To a large extent, the final exam identifies the desired result for content knowledge. Moreover, the syllabus lays out how the content will be covered to get to that result. However, the theory of backward design goes beyond content coverage to focus on what students should be able to do with that information to establish proficiency.

There is no doubt that students must master the rules of the subject-matter area. But because the course is not primarily about rote memorization, knowing the rules is only the start. Students must be able to *do* something with that information to establish proficiency.

Legal education has been focused on learning content, with primarily essay questions and multiple-choice questions used to test content learning. This approach puts little focus on the skills needed to do something with the course knowledge. Backward design theory puts the focus on demonstrating competency. Accordingly, professors should consider how students could demonstrate proficiency with the content as it will be used in practice. In other words, what should students be able to do if they understand the content?

Professor Prompts:

Consider one topic covered in one class period. Think about what that topic looks like in practice, considering the context in which the issue arises and the complications that generally come with the client. Consider the following:

- What skills are needed for the attorney to determine the client's goal?
- What skills does the lawyer need to help the client achieve that goal?
- How can the attorney determine whether there are any internal conflicts in achieving that goal? What skills are needed to resolve them?
- What process would be used to achieve that goal? Document preparation? Negotiation? Litigation? What skills are needed to employ that process?
- What skills are needed to identify specific facts necessary to achieve the client's goal?
- Are there any ethical issues? What skills are needed to resolve them?

Keeping in mind the variety of practical issues an attorney must have the skills to address, consider how those skills might become part of your course instruction. With a clear idea of those skills, consider the three steps of a backward design approach to the course. If it is easier, you could focus on one topic or one class period.

Professor Prompts:

Consider one topic covered in one class period:

1. What do you expect your students to understand before the class is over?
2. What do you expect students to be able to *do* with that knowledge?
3. How can students demonstrate that they can do what you expect them to be able to do?

Plan the class to meet those goals.

When you are ready, you can approach the entire course by considering the three stages from the backward design approach. If it is helpful, in designing the course you can consider the following questions.

Professor Prompts:

On the last day of the course, what will you expect your students to have learned?

- What content area should they have mastered?
- What skills will they need to demonstrate understanding of the content area?
- What skills will they need to provide legal services to a client with an issue in this area once they begin the practice of law?
- To what extent does developing skills to practice in that area of law assist with their understanding of the subject matter?

Once you have a clear idea of where you intend your students to end up, you can begin designing the path for how to get them there.

B. Scaffolding

Scaffolding refers to the process of modeling or demonstrating how to solve a problem, then allowing students to try for themselves, offering assistance as needed. What is being demonstrated to students should be something just beyond what they already know.

For example, when teaching children to read, no instructor would just hand them novels. Rather, the instructor has a series of steps for teaching children. First, they learn the alphabet. Next, they learn short words. The complexity of the words and the story increases over time, and students advance to picture books, chapter books, and beyond.

In the same way, scaffolding can be used in law school to help students build their knowledge. It is a rare student who can, without instruction, read a complex Constitutional law case and fully appreciate the holding. By using scaffolding, professors begin with something students understand and move outward from there, allowing students to try what has been modeled and providing assistance as needed.

Professor Prompts:

Consider one topic covered in one class period:

1. Identify one difficult problem students will be expected to resolve.
2. To eventually be able to solve that problem, what problem must students initially be able to resolve?
3. Begin with the initial easier problem, modeling or demonstrating how to solve successively more difficult problems.
4. Allow students to try to solve the problem on their own, providing assistance as needed.

Scaffolding involves modeling or demonstrating how to solve a problem and assisting students in trying. To this end, consider whether the following might be useful in your course.

1. Demonstrate to students by showing them the process.
2. Verbalize the process by which you are solving a problem.
3. Ask students to share their understanding of the concept, having them relate the new information to something they already understand, which shows that they understand the concept in context.
4. Have students talk about the material and their understanding of it, demonstrating their understanding by being able to articulate the concepts.
5. Ask students to solve a problem, verbalizing their thought process as they move through the problem, while you provide assistance.
6. Use visual aids that represent the ideas you are trying to convey, focusing on organization, sequencing, cause and effect, etc. The visual aid is a tool to guide and shape thinking, not a representation of the result.

C. Knowledge and Skill Transfer

Transfer is students' ability to extend what they have learned in one context to new contexts. The concept of transfer can be used when one set of concepts is transferred to another, from one course to another, from one year to another, and from the classroom to the practice of law. For example, students who learn in Torts that negligence requires a showing of a duty, a breach of that duty, the breach being the cause of damages, and the existence of damages, can transfer that knowledge to other courses in which liability can result from breach of a duty.

Students must first achieve a threshold of learning that is sufficient to support transfer. Spending a lot of time on a subject is not, by itself, sufficient to ensure effective learning. It takes students time to gain familiarity with the subject matter. However, what is more important than the amount of time students spend is *how* they spend that time. As students work, they should evaluate their level of understanding, not simply be reading and rereading the text or an outline.

Learning with understanding is more likely to allow students to transfer the knowledge than simply memorizing information. Students develop a flexible understanding of when, where, and how to use the knowledge to solve new problems if they have learned how to extract underlying themes and concepts from the material. More specifically, once students have gained a sufficient understanding of information, they can begin to see it applied in other contexts.

From the professor's perspective, one classroom will look no different from another classroom if the only measure of learning is students' memorization of facts and rules. That information will be "context-bound" because it is seen only in the context-specific examples and applications of that course. In contrast, one classroom will be different from the other classrooms if the measure of learning includes students' ability to transfer what they learned to new problems and settings.

When information is organized and presented in a conceptual framework, students will better be able to see how information learned in one class can be transferred to another. With an understanding of how the information fits into the framework, students can shift that concept to a new context, learning the information more quickly. Seeing the information presented in several contexts, students become even more likely to be able to extract the relevant features of the concepts and develop a more flexible representation of knowledge that can be used more generally. For example, damages is a concept that appears in many classes and under a variety of circumstances. Once students learn foundational information about damages, the area becomes more nuanced as they see how it is applied in their Contracts or Business Organizations or Property or Constitutional Law class.

Transfer of learning is an active process. Student have to learn initial information. They then begin to see how that information appears in other contexts. Often, there is no direct evidence of the impact of transfer until students realize that they were able to grasp new information more quickly. The most effective learning happens when students transfer what they have learned to various and diverse new situations.

The same concept that applies to knowledge transfer applies to skills transfer. The more students begin to learn lawyering skills, the more they can transfer and apply them to new situations. Professors in second- and third-year courses can leverage skills learned in the first year by showing how those same skills are relevant in their course. The repetition not only reinforces the skills, but demonstrates new ways in which the skills can be used. For example, what begins as the skill of interviewing a client can lead to the skill of interviewing a potential witness and then to the skill of taking a deposition.

Professor Prompts:

Consider your course:

Knowledge:
1. Identify a concept from your course that appears in another course.
2. If students have taken the other course, can you connect the knowledge from that course to your course?
3. If students will take the other course in the future, can you lay the foundation for the transfer of knowledge from your course to the future course?

Skills:
1. Identify a skill you expect your students to learn in your course. Identify another course that requires the same skill.
2. If students have taken the other course, can you connect the use of the skill in the other course to use of the skill in your course?
3. If students will take the other course in the future, can you lay the foundation for the transfer of the skill from your course to the future course?

D. Bloom's Taxonomy

Bloom's Taxonomy of Cognitive Objectives is a skills-based taxonomy, specifically designed to establish whether learners have attained acceptable skills as targeted in learning outcomes. The lowest skill level is knowledge and basic comprehension. From there, students move up through the levels, with each new level incorporating the skills required at the lower levels and adding more demanding intellectual behaviors. The taxonomy informs the process by which students acquire increasingly refined skills.

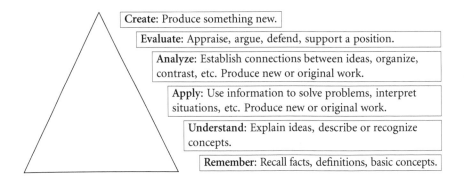

Create: Produce something new.

Evaluate: Appraise, argue, defend, support a position.

Analyze: Establish connections between ideas, organize, contrast, etc. Produce new or original work.

Apply: Use information to solve problems, interpret situations, etc. Produce new or original work.

Understand: Explain ideas, describe or recognize concepts.

Remember: Recall facts, definitions, basic concepts.

The level within the taxonomy will inform the level of *doing* required of students. At the lower levels, students must demonstrate basic content knowledge. For example, students may be expected to apply specific rules to a fact pattern. If students are sufficiently progressed within the taxonomy, they may be expected to demonstrate the ability to evaluate the strength of a client's position.

With the taxonomy as a guide, professors can intentionally craft a learning process that assists students in moving from the lowest level of the taxonomy to the highest level, or at least the highest that reasonably can be expected. Professors can focus on how students could demonstrate their learning and can structure the course to prepare students to carry out that demonstration. Professors should also remember that skills development requires practice. To move up the taxonomy, students need time to engage with the material in ways that extend beyond reading the assignment and to the skills they need to apply the knowledge they are gaining.

Consider how to build skills in your course through the steps of Bloom's Taxonomy:

Remember	What is the basic knowledge students must possess to understand the rules?
Understand	How will you know whether students comprehend the basic knowledge needed to understand the area?
Apply	How can students demonstrate their knowledge and comprehension?
Analyze	Can students use what they have learned to solve a problem?
Evaluate and Create	Can students see beyond what they have been taught to devise new solutions or applications of the law?

Chapter 2

Assessment, Feedback, and Calibration

Assessment works on two levels: first, it shows students what they don't know, and second, it shows professors what students don't know. Research shows that long-term learning occurs only when students develop habits for figuring out what they understand and, perhaps more importantly, what they don't understand. Only by making mistakes can students connect important pieces of the learning puzzle. Professors can help students make these connections by giving them opportunities to assess. Assessment also allows professors opportunities to determine what students are and are not understanding. With frequent assessment, both teacher and student can calibrate the learning process, promoting longer-term learning.

Since 2014, the ABA has required law schools to "utilize both formative and summative assessment methods in its curriculum to measure and improve student learning and provide meaningful feedback to students." (Standard 314) Standard 314 works in conjunction with Standard 302, also adopted in 2014, requiring law schools to establish minimum competency outcomes. Traditionally, law schools assessed student learning only at the end of a course—either after a semester or an entire academic year—through final exams. Today's law school faculty are required to assess much more frequently.

> **Professor Prompts:**
>
> - What are the different types of assessments you can create?
> - What, exactly, should be assessed?
> - What do you do with the information you receive after an assessment?

A. Formative and Summative Assessments

Assessments do not necessarily occur as exams or tests. Exams are only one way to assess: there are many others. Assessments should not be thought of as rare, high-stakes performance, but as frequent student activities. They can range from optional to required, or from ungraded to low-points to high-stakes opportunities for students to perform. Assessments can take as little as a few minutes to as much as several hours. They might require extensive, individualized grading and feedback from professors, or they might be evaluated by peers, or they might be graded by teaching assistants, or they might be automatically graded by a computer. In short, an assessment can be of any size or shape.

Assessments generally fall into one of two categories: formative or summative. A formative assessment primarily serves to inform student and professor what concepts need additional attention. The fundamental purpose of such an assessment is to find gaps in understanding so that instruction and study habits can be altered to fill those gaps.

> **Professor Prompts:**
>
> - What steps do you take throughout the term to understand what your students are learning?
> - How often do you take those steps?
> - What do you do if students are not learning what you think they are learning?

In contrast, a summative assessment primarily serves to benchmark individual students against pre-determined competencies. The fundamental purpose of a summative assessment is to classify how much understanding a student developed by the end of an instructional period. Because law school education is cumulative, even summative assessments, especially in the first year of law school, can be used in a formative way—that is, to help students improve in future courses and to pass the bar exam (the ultimate summative assessment).

Professor Prompts:

- When do you give a summative assessment?
- What are your expectations about student performance on the assessment?
- How were those expectations formed?
- Do your students know what your expectations are?

All formative assessments require professors to provide useful feedback so that students can calibrate or adjust their study to improve learning. Feedback comes in many varieties as well, but feedback always needs the following components.

Preparation to accept feedback. Students must be prepared to accept feedback. There are several ways to help students be receptive. First, professors can explain to students why constructive feedback is important to the learning process and how significant learning takes place when students make mistakes, understand their mistakes, and then adjust their study approaches to what they have learned. Professors can normalize the idea that learning should feel difficult, at least some of the time, and that struggling to understand something is often a sign of real learning. When students believe the reason a professor is giving feedback is to help students achieve excellence—and that such excellence is attainable—they are receptive to it. Second, professors can involve students in self-diagnosis, a process that helps both students and professor see how to help students improve. Third, professors can help students appreciate when their performance is good so that they can maintain motivation and consciously repeat things that they are doing right.

Feedback should include a diagnosis. Feedback has to show students what they got right or wrong; it must include a diagnosis. At its core, useful feedback is a specific diagnosis. The professor's task is to show students how their product fails to meet a standard. The more specific the feedback, the more it helps students to fix the problem. For example, assume that a student produced a "B" answer on an essay. Why was this a "B" answer? The notation "pretty good" does not help the student see what was missing. The student may have missed one or more of the issues. Which one(s)? Or the student may have failed to state rules clearly and consistently. Or the student may have spotted all the issues and produced perfect "general rule" statements, but failed to indicate exceptions to the rules. Or the student may have failed to apply the facts to the rules. Or the student may have failed to argue both sides of a close question. Another student might get the same grade, but maybe that student did not use correct terminology, or the essay's structure was confusing and hard to follow. These are all different problems. Students need to know which problem they have. The feedback should be as specific as possible.

Feedback should include a remedy. Feedback has to contain attainable and clear standards for how to achieve excellence, i.e., a remedy for the problem that was diagnosed. The professor should assist the student in outlining a re-medial plan. What will the student do differently the next time, and how will the student achieve that result? For example, the professor might suggest to a student who has sparse or imprecise rule statements to go back and outline the major topics for the class. Then, to check the result, the professor could give the student optional short-answer quizzes. Another student might need to practice writing out the structure for how to approach that problem, being sure to list the major rules, elements, tests, factors and exceptions. The student should practice the same type of problem several times, always being careful to recite the proper rule structure, going back and checking to see whether she remembered all the components. For a student who produced a very weak essay, the professor might suggest that the student re-write and re-submit the same essay for review. If the original essay was well-written, the professor might suggest that the student practice old exam essays and turn one in for review and additional feedback. Students should clearly understand the professor's grading rubric and what each component should look like. Each student's problem may require a different remedy.

B. What Should Be Assessed

1. Assess What Students Know and Do Not Know

Even experienced professors might struggle with how much time to devote to particular concepts. Ideally, they should focus more time on concepts that students struggle to understand, and less time on concepts students have little trouble grasping (factoring in the relative importance of the concepts as they relate to learning outcomes). Because students come to courses with different levels of understanding, finding this balance can be hard.

Early assessments can help professors understand what students know even before they begin a particular course or unit. Such assessments can be quick and frequent, helping gauge how much or how little to focus on a particular topic or idea. These assessments are always formative because students are just beginning to learn the concepts. Some examples of these formative assessments include:

- Professor-designed questions on a learning management system, either as a threaded discussion or stand-alone questions, asking students to discuss concepts in the assigned reading material.
- Professor-designed questions presented in class via polling or one-minute essays.
- Short-definition sheets or short hypotheticals asking students to make educated guesses about material not yet studied.
- Practice exercises that review both concepts already studied and new concepts. This practice, called interleaving, enhances long-term retention.

Formative assessments help students build mental structures that they can use to process new concepts when they embark on more in-depth study. In addition, the assessments identify student misconceptions that could get in the way of learning.

2. Feedback on Learning

After covering material, it is critical that students understand what they learned and did not learn. Encouraging students to recall information, make mistakes, and then fix those mistakes can foster long-term learning.

Students need to practice retrieval of concepts from memory, at spaced intervals, to see for themselves what they do and do not understand. Professors should offer students opportunities to test themselves regularly, and at spaced intervals. These self-guided assessments can be optional or required and can be set up in a variety of ways that offer students a chance to see the answers immediately after completing the assessment. These assessments are always formative because the purpose is for students to adjust, or calibrate, their study based on the results. Examples of these types of assessments include:

- Short-answer quizzes. These quizzes can be housed in a learning management system or given on paper at the end or beginning of class, and the correct answers should be made available immediately after the quiz. Students can be allowed to take the quizzes as often as they want and at different times during the term.

- Multiple-choice exams. These exams can be housed in a learning management system that offers the correct answers immediately after taking the quiz. Students can be allowed to take the exams as many times as they want and at different times during the term.
- Mixing material already studied with new material (interleaving) to help students retain concepts.
- In-class polling, which offers immediate feedback to students.
- In-class exercises, reviewing concepts learned, with in-class debriefing of answers. This exercise provides immediate feedback to students. In-class exercises can be conducted in pairs, in groups, by the entire class at once, or by offering students a choice of solo or collaborative participation.

3. Understanding What Is Not Understood

When helping students take charge of their own learning, professors must help students understand what they do and do not understand and how to adjust their learning.

In addition to the self-guided assessments discussed above, professors can give assessments that are followed by individualized feedback. In the self-guided assessments described above, students compare their answers to pre-programmed responses written in advance by the professor. But another type of assessment is one that allows a professor, teaching assistant, or peer to give individualized feedback on student performance. While there might be a summative component to this assessment (e.g., a midterm essay), the primary purpose is formative. Such assessments can include:

- Practice essays submitted to a professor, teaching assistant, or peer. The grader compares the essay to a standardized rubric, diagnosing problem areas, and suggesting remedial action. Individual meetings can enhance the efficacy of this type of assessment.
- Graded essays. These essays would be similar to the practice essays above, but would count toward the final grade.
- A series of peer-edited essays. Students would be required to peer-edit multiple peers' work, following a carefully constructed rubric. Students can re-write their original essay based on feedback from three or four peers.

- In-class exercises where the professor monitors the process and offers solutions to problems, suggesting corrective action in the moment.
- Significant out-of-class assignments, such as drafting exercises, reacting to a video, or simulation assignments.

4. Establishing That Students Have Developed Competencies

Students, professors, and the law school need to know whether students have developed competencies. ABA Standard 302 requires law schools to develop minimum competency outcomes for students, and each professor should develop course objectives for each course. Ultimately, professors are responsible for awarding grades based on how well students achieve the course objectives. Grades are typically based on a combination of scores earned on formative assessments plus scores earned on one or more summative assessments. Traditionally, the prime example of a summative assessment is a final exam. Such an exam might be given once, at the end of the semester. Or, instead of a final exam, there might be several exams given throughout the semester. A summative exam might include:

- Essay questions;
- Short-answer or fill-in-the-blank questions;
- True/false questions;
- Multiple-choice questions;
- An applied exercise such as a drafting exercise or a reaction to a video or simulation; or
- Oral performance.

While the final exam is summative, students in their first year can benefit by getting specific, individualized feedback of the type discussed above. Students should be encouraged to see the professor after reviewing the final exam results. This will give them the benefit of a formative diagnosis and help them to develop new approaches to learning.

C. Using the Information from Assessments

In addition to helping students to calibrate after each assessment—that is, to adjust the way they study and prepare—professors can use assessment data to calibrate their own teaching. Each type of assessment offers professors the opportunity to consider how they might teach the material differently. Just as students need to self-assess, faculty need to self-assess. Using data from student assessments is an excellent way to accomplish this goal. Reviewing student responses to assessments is one of the best ways to look for patterns that might indicate gaps or other instances of less-than-effective teaching. If a significant group of students get something wrong in the same way, professors should look for a different way to teach that material to address the misunderstandings.

This book includes numerous assessment activities. They follow the general guidelines discussed above.

Chapter 3

Being Intentional about the Process: How Are Students Learning?

Professors know the law they teach. That knowledge extends not only to subject matter (and its place in the larger context of the law), but also to how the rules are organized. Within that organization, they understand the hierarchy of the rules, being able to touch on the most important rules with ease. They can identify which areas of law are well settled, which are subject to change, which are applied most often, and which are implicated rarely. They can break the area down and see pockets of rules, with each pocket containing a cluster of rules congregating around one or two main ideas.

This knowledge allows professors to effectively and efficiently address a fact pattern. The most important facts come to the forefront, with the remainder falling away. Commonplace and expected facts are distinguished from atypical and unexpected facts. Facts that require a certain conclusion are separated from facts that might support a different result.

Professors coalesce the relevant facts into a meaningful pattern that they then overlay with the relevant pocket of rules. They apply only those rules, considering the internal hierarchy and complement of supporting rules, and reach a conclusion. All this happens without professors giving much conscious thought to their process.

Students, in contrast, are novices who are not able to do any (or most) of those things—at least in that subject-matter area of the law.

Starting from such disparate places, a lot must happen before students can begin to apply the law anywhere near as effectively and efficiently as professors. Memorizing and understanding the rules is important and an integral part of something larger—the learning process. To this end, students must appreciate that more is expected of them than memorizing rules and case holdings. Similarly, professors should appreciate that just telling or showing students rules and case holdings does little to help students develop a process or framework for applying the law.

Learning the law is like learning to build a house. The professor could show students pictures of a variety of houses, comparing and contrasting styles, amenities, structural challenges, etc. While looking at the pictures, the professor would understand all the intricacies behind each design. However, students see only a single picture and what the professor points out about that picture. While certainly helpful, this approach (looking at pictures of completed houses) does little to teach students much about the process of building a house.

> **Professor Prompt:**
>
> Can you connect what you are doing in the classroom to a specific process needed to apply the law?

People learn by connecting what they are learning to what they already know. With this in mind, professors should meet students where they are and build from there. That means starting at the beginning.

A. Policy

With few exceptions, students begin each course with a blank slate. They will neither appreciate the nuances of the content area, nor perceive an organizational structure. All pieces of information have the same potential to be important, and they appear to be random.

To begin organizing and understanding the area, students need a framework around which they can structure learning and knowledge. In law school, the widest lens is the policy that drives the area of the law. When students understand the policy behind the law, and how the rule is intended to be fair, it will be easier for them to see how the rules support (or don't support) the policy objective.

For example, when building a house, there are at least two overarching policy objectives. First, the house must provide shelter. Beyond that basic requirement, the house can provide certain functional amenities. Second, the house must be constructed so that it is safe to inhabit. Safety is achieved by a series of requirements applied to the plumbing and electrical systems, foundation construction, structural support, etc.

Professor Prompts:

1. What overarching policy do the laws support?
2. How do the laws work to support that policy?
3. Does the policy embody a sense of fairness?
4. Could the policy be seen by some as unfair?

How students understand the policy can be influenced by personal experience. Some may begin class with incorrect ideas of policies or enactment of those policies. These ideas can influence how students interpret the material, causing them either to not understand or to misunderstand the material. For example, if students grew up where homes regularly had not been built to code, unsafe houses may have been an accepted norm. When learning about safety rules, they may be thinking:

- The rules are a farce and do not reflect what really happens.
- The rules do not achieve the intended standard of safety.
- The rules are optional. Clearly, not all houses are constructed in a manner that satisfies the rules.

If professors are unaware of students' preconceptions, they will not get addressed and can get in the way of students' learning.

Professor Prompts:

1. In what situations is the policy clearly not being achieved?
2. Why is the policy not being achieved?
3. Is there an explanation for the breach between the policy and what is actually happening?
4. Does that breach need to be eliminated?

B. The Core: Definitions, Rules, and Contextual Understanding

1. The Basics

Critical thinking is impossible if the thinker does not clearly understand what to be thinking about. Accordingly, starting at the beginning means starting with the core around which the specific content area is built. Definitions and rules form this core. These definitions and rules, once understood, work together to create basic concepts that students can use as a framework for understanding going forward. There is no area of law that does not have certain words, rules, and basic concepts that students must understand to be able to comprehend the assigned reading, a court opinion, the material presented during this class period, and material to be presented during the next class period.

Having identified the policy framework behind house construction, the professor can move toward demonstrating how the policies are baked into the law and how they govern the various steps needed to build the house. If professors want to meet students where they are, professors must begin at the most basic level. For example, explaining that plastic pipes were used when copper pipes should have been used will likely be lost on students who do not understand what the pipes will be used for, where they were in the house, and the pros and cons of copper and plastic pipes. They have no framework for understanding and no structure to which to attach the knowledge.

Professor Prompts:

Consider just one class period or one topic to be covered in one class period:

1. Identify three words students must understand to comprehend the material you will present.
2. Identify the rule(s) connected to the identified words students must understand.
3. Identify the basic concept(s) students are to recognize by knowing the identified words and rules.

Even though definitions, rules, and concepts are the most fundamental of building blocks, most professors spend little to no time discussing them. The traditional view is that students should learn the definitions and rules on their own, without the assistance of the professor. That is why students have a textbook, assigned cases, and supplements.

This approach has three fundamental problems. First, the professor is demonstrating for students what is important. If professors fail to spend time discussing and reflecting on the definitions, rules, and concepts, students will follow this lead and spend little time on them as well. Instead, their focus will be where the professor's focus is—on briefing cases and summarizing holdings. Unfortunately, students can summarize a case holding without truly understanding the rule the court applied to reach its result.

Second, telling students that they need to learn the definitions, rules, and concepts isn't as important as helping them to understand whether they have actually learned them. In short, students can believe they have learned something when they haven't. Nuances and characteristics often hide in the shadows, away from the students' focus. It is impossible for students to appreciate these subtle aspects when they haven't even realized that they exist.

Moreover, students' understanding something told to them is different than their knowing it in a way that they can use in the future. For example, a student can understand a joke he hears on Monday, but not be able to tell it to his friends that weekend. Similarly, a student can understand the professor's lecture, but not know the content in a way that allows him to apply it in future classes. Unfortunately, unless this misconception is corrected, the student believes that, because he understands the reading and lecture, he has sufficiently learned the material. Because he will be the one practicing law, the student needs to be the one who can tell the joke.

Professor Prompts:

Consider the definitions, rules, and concepts to be covered in one class period or in one topic in that class period:

1. Which definitions, rules, or concepts will appear in a topic covered in a future class?
2. Is the definition, rule, or concept one that students struggle with?
3. How do you know whether students are struggling with a definition, rule, or concept?

Third, professors believe and expect that students are learning the definitions, rules, and concepts on their own. Students, being human, often take the path of least resistance. If they can put off learning definitions and laws until tomorrow, or better yet, until they study for the final exam, they will. The result is that students are reading assignments and listening to lectures without a full grasp of the nuances of words, the subtle implications of rules, or how concepts can appear in cases.

For example, in the course on house construction, the professor may have explained the difference between plastic pipes and copper pipes, covering the functional and physical differences and the pros and cons. However, if students have not internalized the differences, the professor's showing pictures of different houses and commenting on which ones used copper pipes and which used plastic will have little significance. The professor can keep lecturing, but the reality is that students' ability to learn is severely compromised, except on a most superficial level.

Professor Prompts:

Consider the definitions, rules, and concepts to be covered in one class period or in one topic in that class period:

1. How do you know whether students understand the definitions, rules, and concepts?
2. How do you know whether students have internalized the information in such a way that they can use it in the future?
3. Will students' learning going forward be compromised if they haven't internalized the knowledge today?

Of course, there is a fourth possibility. Students could, in fact, know the definitions, rules, and concepts in a way that encompasses understanding and goes beyond, allowing them to use the information. If that is truly the case, the professor can move directly to the next building block. But in such instances, there is no harm, and a lot of benefit, in validating for students their level of knowledge.

Alternative Approach to Covering a Case: Rather than approaching a case using IRAC, expect students to view the case from the perspective of the "R." Students must identify the definitions and specific rules applied by the court, starting with the most general and moving progressively to the most specific. Where appropriate, they should address rules the court might have, but chose not to, apply.

Class discussion of the case also should be from the perspective of the rules. For example:

1. Why did the court rely on those rules?
2. How were those rules implicated by the facts?
3. Did the court apply the rules in an expected way?
4. Could the court have applied those rules and reached a different result? How?

---

2. Assessment Suggestions

Feedback is vital for the students. Without feedback, they don't know what they don't know. An assessment is a means of checking in with students, determining whether they understand the information, and reflecting back to them what they understand and what they don't.

For example, students in the class on house construction might receive feedback on whether two-by-fours were properly placed. As this is a core requirement in creating a safe house, this information is vital. The assessment also informs the professor as to what information has been learned and what hasn't. If the two-by-fours were not properly placed, the professor should consider further instruction in that area.

> **Assessment Suggestions:** Core knowledge comes in layers of complexity. An assessment can be directed to any of these layers, depending on the professor's goal. The following suggestions are arranged from lower-order tasks to higher-order tasks.
>
> 1. Give a multiple-choice quiz on the most important definitions used during that class session. The quiz can be administered before class, during class, or after class. There are many resources that allow quizzes to be automatically scored, providing both the professor and students with immediate feedback.
> 2. Require students to write a definition, state a rule, or explain a concept in their own words.
> 3. Require students to explain in writing an application of a rule or concept in a way that demonstrates a clear understanding of the concept.

3. Exercises for Focusing on Core Information

- The following is a list of prompts you could use to probe whether students understand a definition, rule, or concept:

Definitions	How would you define _____? How would you identify _____? How would you recognize _____? How would you clarify the meaning of _____?
Rules	How would you state the rule regarding _____? How could you express _____? How could you describe _____? How would you differentiate between _____ and _____? What are the major elements of _____?
Concepts	How could you describe _____? What is the main idea of _____? What could you say about _____? Could you restate _____? How would you explain _____?

- The following is an exercise that you could use to identify the definitions, rules, and concepts to focus on during a class and to begin thinking about how to determine whether students understand and have internalized them:

Definitions				
What are the three most important words students should be able to define to understand the material to be covered in that class period?	Why are these words important?	How could you check to verify that one student knows the definitions?	How could you check to verify that three students know the definitions?	How could you check to verify that all students know the definitions?
Rules				
What are the two most important rules students should be able to recite to be able to apply them to a fact pattern?	Why are these rules important?	How could you verify that one student can recite the rules?	How could you verify that three students can recite the rules?	How could you verify that all students can recite the rules?
Concepts				
What is the most important concept you will cover in class?	Why is it the most important concept?	How could you verify that one student understands the concept?	How can you verify that three students understand the concept?	How can you verify that all students understand the concept?

C. Chunking Information

1. Understanding Chunking

Short-term (i.e., working) memory can manipulate on average only seven pieces of information at a time. When short-term memory is at capacity, any additional information cannot be processed or stored. It falls out or disappears.

When individual pieces of information are organized (chunked) into a larger unit or a familiar pattern, that larger unit becomes a more powerful piece of information available for use by the student's short-term memory. Moreover, when information is chunked together, the grouped information holds more meaning and becomes easier to recall.

Example:

Can you remember this number?
  2075554694
Can you remember this number more easily? Why?
  207-555-4694

Chess is one example where chunking is very important. Chess masters organize strategic patterns of moves involving certain pieces. Novices do not yet see the game as containing specific possible patterns. By chunking, experts can anticipate more possible outcomes deriving from one move. They determine their next move based on that information.

Quote:

In one study, a chess master, a Class A player (good but not a master), and a novice were given 5 seconds to view a chess board position from the middle of a chess game. After 5 seconds the board was covered, and each participant attempted to reconstruct the board position on another board. This procedure was repeated for multiple trials until everyone received a perfect score. On the first trial, the master player correctly placed many more pieces than the Class A player, who in turn placed more than the novice.

However, these results occurred only when the chess pieces were arranged in configurations that conformed to meaningful games of chess. When chess pieces were randomized and presented for 5 seconds, the recall of the chess master and Class A player were the same as the novice.

National Research Council, How PEOPLE LEARN, Ch. 2., *How Experts Differ From Novices*, p. 35.

Chunking can be done using different approaches. First, information can be chunked into small groups that make it easier to remember. (See the telephone number example above.) Second, information can be chunked into patterns that repeat themselves. This is the type of chunking used by chess players. Finally, information can be chunked based on meaning. For example, a random list of foods can be organized into categories like fruits, vegetables, breads, and meats. Or the categories might be based on what meal the foods would be served at (breakfast, lunch, dinner, snack); or the categories might be based on where the items would be found in the grocery store (produce, dairy, paper products, cleaning products).

If the information is chunked into pieces that are too small, the learning becomes repetitive and little information processing benefit is gained. If the information is chunked into chunks that are too large, the chunk cannot be recalled and learning is frustrated.

Professor Prompts:

Consider the information to be covered over one week:

1. Is there a pattern to facts presented in the cases? Is the pattern important?
2. Is there a pattern to how the court applies the rules? Is that pattern important or accidental?
3. Can facts be grouped into categories? Is there a benefit to grouping them?
4. Can the rules be grouped into categories? How are the categories determined?
5. Can the class information be broken into and presented in segments?

As an expert in the area, the professor is already chunking information, most likely without even being conscious of doing so. Students, not yet able to do the same, are processing a case or a problem using a much smaller amount of information, often arriving at an erroneous or incomplete conclusion, and taking more time to get there.

When students have learned the definitions, rules, and concepts, they are ready to begin chunking this information. Of course, if students have not learned the core information, they cannot begin the process of chunking.

Alternative Approach to Covering a Case: Rather than approaching a case using IRAC, expect students to identify patterns in the case. Class discussion of the case also should be from the perspective of the patterns. For example:

1. Do the facts follow a pattern similar to previous cases covered?
2. Could you alter the pattern of facts in such a way that you would expect the court to reach a different result?
3. Is there a pattern to how the court applied the rules? Is the pattern important?
4. Could the court have used a different pattern of rules to reach a different result? If so, why did it select the pattern that it did?

For a chunk of information to solidify, students should understand application of the chunk in the context in which it will be used and be given the opportunity to practice using the chunk. Repetition and practice are necessary to shift the chunk from working memory to the unconscious, giving students the space to move to a higher level of thinking.

2. Assessment Suggestions

Feedback is vital for students. Without feedback, they don't know what they don't know. An assessment is a means of checking in with students, determining whether they understand the information, and reflecting back to them what they understand and what they don't.

For example, students in the class on house construction might receive feedback on whether they understand chunks of information such as the basic elements of the electrical system or the standards for structural integrity. The assessment also informs the professor as to what information has been learned and what hasn't. If students aren't recognizing information as belonging in groups, the professor should consider further instruction in that area.

Assessment Suggestions: Chunking can start small, with the amount of information being chunked increasing as understanding increases. The following are suggestions for determining whether students have begun chunking information:

1. Require students to identify three rules that are often applied together. Have them explain how the rules are connected.
2. Give students a fact pattern and have them identify the five most important facts. Have them state whether they had a specific rule in mind when selecting the most important facts.
3. Require students to submit an outline they prepared covering a specific, discrete topic.

---

3. Exercises for Focusing on Chunking

The following is an exercise that you could use to help identify information that could be chunked.

Considering the information to be covered in a class period:		
What information do you expect students to chunk together? Will the chunking be by groups, patterns, or meaning?	What would trigger students to notice that a chunk of information should be used?	Will students be expected to draw upon chunks from previous classes?

Chapter 3 Workbook

Being Intentional about the Process: How Are Students Learning?

I. Work for the Professor

BACKGROUND

Course: _____

Types of practice areas (e.g., litigation, planning, transactional, regulatory):

1. _____

2. _____

3. _____

4. _____

Considering the practice areas identified above, can you connect them to the topics you cover and the method by which you cover the topics?

	Practice Area	Course Topics	Connection
1.			
2.			
3.			
4.			

POLICY

The rules of a subject-matter area often can be more easily understood if the policy behind them is made clear. With that in mind, consider the following broad issues related to the policy behind the rules of your course:

Policy: Part I

1.	What is the broadest policy statement that drives the rules in this area?	
2.	Have students been exposed to this type of policy in the past? If yes, in what ways? If no, how can you help them relate to the policy?	
3.	How does the policy drive the rules?	
4.	Does the policy change depending on which political party is in office? Why?	
5.	Is the policy fair to everyone?	
6.	Will there be some who view the policy as unfair?	
7.	Can the view that the policy is fair by some and unfair by others be reconciled?	

How students understand the policy can be influenced by personal experience. Some students may begin class with incorrect ideas about policies or the impact of those policies. These ideas can influence how students interpret the material presented, causing them either not to understand or to misunderstand the material. Taking into consideration the possible perspectives of your students, consider the following questions:

Policy: Part II

1.	How might your students have experienced the policy?	
2.	In what ways might your students misunderstand the policy?	
3.	Could there be a disconnect between the policy and its impact on individuals?	

Sometimes there is a disconnect between the policy objective and what the rules are actually achieving. With that issue in mind, consider the following:

Policy: Part III

1.	In what situations is the policy not clearly being achieved?	
2.	Why isn't the policy being achieved?	
3.	What is the reason for the disconnect?	
4.	Can that disconnect be remedied?	

II. Each Class Period

A worksheet should be completed for each class period and each major topic covered in that class period.

Class Period: _____

Topics to Be Covered:

1. _____

2. _____

3. _____

Considering each of the topics separately, complete the following charts:

Basics:

1.	What three words must students understand to comprehend the material?	
2.	What two rules must students understand?	
3.	What one concept do the words and rules convey?	
4.	How will you know whether students understand the words, rules, and concepts?	
5.	If students do not understand the words, rules, and concepts, in what areas are they likely to struggle later in the course?	

When individual pieces of information are organized (chunked) into a larger unit or a familiar pattern, that larger unit becomes a more powerful piece of information available for use by students' short-term memory. Moreover, when information is chunked together, the grouped information holds more meaning and becomes easier to recall. You could use the following chart to help you plan a lesson on chunking:

Chunking:

• What information can be organized into small groups so that it is easier to remember?	
• What relevant facts usually occur together?	
• What group of small rules is often applied in a set pattern or order?	
• What information can be grouped based on meaning or use?	
• What information can be grouped because it fits into a specific category?	
• Identify opportunities where you could demonstrate to students the chunking of information.	
• Identify opportunities that would allow students to practice chunking information.	
• Identify opportunities that would allow students to see the chunked material in context.	
• In which future classes will the chunked information be useful?	

III. Assessments for Students

Understanding the Basics:

Alternative Approach to Covering a Case: Rather than approaching a case using IRAC, expect students to view the case from the perspective of the "R." Students must identify the definitions and specific rules applied by the court, starting with the most general and moving progressively to the most specific. Where appropriate, they should address rules the court might have, but chose not to, apply.

Class discussion of the case also should be from the perspective of the rules. For example:

1. Why did the court rely on those rules?
2. How were those rules implicated by the facts?
3. Did the court apply the rules in an expected way?
4. Could the court have applied those rules and reached a different result? How?

Assessment Suggestions: Core knowledge comes in layers of complexity. An assessment can be directed to any of these layers, depending on the goal of the professor. The following suggestions are arranged from lower-order tasks to higher-order tasks.

1. Give a multiple-choice quiz on the most important definitions used during that class session. The quiz can be administered before class, during class, or after class. There are many resources that allow quizzes to be automatically scored, providing both the professor and students with immediate feedback.
2. Require students to write a definition, state a rule, or explain a concept in their own words.
3. Require students to explain in writing an application of a rule or concept in a way that demonstrates a clear understanding of the concept.

Ask students the following (whether in writing, orally in class, having students respond using clickers, etc.), with the professor filling in the blanks:

Definitions	How would you define _____? How would you identify _____? How would you recognize _____? How would you clarify the meaning of _____?
Rules	How would you state the rule regarding _____? How could you express _____? How could you describe _____? How would you differentiate between _____ and _____? What are the major elements of _____?
Concepts	How could you describe _____? What is the main idea of _____? What could you say about _____? Could you restate _____? How would you explain _____?

Chunking information can help students learn, understand, and apply a subject-matter area.

Alternative Approach to Covering a Case: Rather than approaching a case using IRAC, expect students to identify patterns in the case. Class discussion of the case also should reflect the patterns. For example:

1. Do the facts follow a pattern similar to previous cases covered?
2. Could you alter the pattern of facts in such a way that you would expect the court to reach a different result?
3. Is there a pattern to how the court applied the rules? Is the pattern important?
4. Could the court have used a different pattern of rules to reach a different result? If so, why did it select the pattern it did?

Assessment Suggestions: Chunking can start small, with the amount of information being chunked increasing as understanding increases. The following are suggestions for determining whether students have begun chunking information.

1. Require students to identify three rules that are often applied together. Have them explain how the rules are connected.
2. Give students a fact pattern and have them identify the five most important facts. Have them state whether they had a specific rule in mind when selecting the most important facts.
3. Require students to submit an outline they prepared covering a specific, discrete topic.

Chapter 4

Fully Understanding the Client's Problem

Because doctrinal courses are usually taught through a combination of appellate cases and short hypothetical problems, students often miss the centrality, to lawyers, of the client's goals. Not all law school graduates represent clients, but most do. Law schools today want to educate students to become ethical practitioners of law. Legal ethics rules make clear that, in a traditional legal case or controversy, a lawyer cannot act in any important way without understanding the full depth of a client's problem and goals. In fact, ethics rules require attorneys to:

- Understand all of the goals clients want to achieve related to their cases;
- Provide all meaningful information to clients about the law and the factors that influence their cases;
- Consult fully and frankly with clients about choices that need to be made and;
- Carry out the goals and choices clients want (except in very limited circumstances).

The attorney-client relationship, under current ethics rules, is both a principal/agent relationship and a fiduciary relationship. That means that lawyers have to work to fulfill their clients' goals (if possible within the constraints of the law), and they also have to protect their clients' interests.

Given the primacy of the attorney-client relationship, all law school courses should help students to understand how legal doctrine arises out of attorney-client relationships, and not just as some separate field unrelated to clients.

There are many ways in a doctrinal classroom to help students see the connection of clients to the acts of lawyers, including:

- When students are first reading appellate cases, ask them to identify the parties and what they were seeking;
- Help students see why attorneys make certain choices in the arguments they raise;
- When students are learning legal doctrine, require them to participate in experiential exercises that put them in a client-like role and;
- Require students to participate in experiential exercises that present them with a more fully realized client than typical short problems offer.

To be clear, most law schools offer second- and third-year courses in specific client-based skills such as interviewing, counseling, negotiation, mediation, and full client representation (clinics). But those classes should not be the first time students connect client goals to legal arguments. After all, for a lawyer, the client is the starting point for virtually every legal case. As one group of educators observed, the experience of clients is something typically missing from law school case-method courses:[1]

> It is noteworthy that throughout legal education, the focus remains on cases rather than clients. The analogy in medical training would be the tension between focusing teaching on disease processes, on the one hand, or on patient care, on the other. The skill of thinking like a lawyer is first learned without the benefit of actual clients, and the typical form in which the case books present cases may even suggest something misleading about the role lawyers play, more often casting them as distant planners or observers than as interactive participants in legal actions.[2]

Appellate cases are several steps removed from clients, where a typical timeline goes something like this:

1. Client meets with lawyer and describes problem;
2. Client retains lawyer if warranted;
3. Lawyer understands client goals;
4. Lawyer evaluates claims/defenses, investigates facts, determines options, describes options;

---

1. WILLIAM M. SULLIVAN, ANNE COLBY, JUDITH WELCH WEGNER, LLOYD BOND & LEE S. SHULMAN, EDUCATING LAWYERS: PREPARATION FOR THE PROFESSION OF LAW 56–57 (2007).
    2. *Id.*

5. Lawyer attempts to resolve dispute outside of litigation (and is often successful);
6. Lawyer files lawsuit/defends if unable to resolve without litigation;
7. Lawyer tries to resolve case through legal non-trial processes (e.g., summary judgment, settlement, or mediation);
8. Lawyer tries case before judge or jury (the number of cases that go to trial is only about 5% of civil cases that reached step #6 and between 5–10% of criminal cases);
9. Lawyer who loses case appeals (appeals constitute about .075% of cases that went into some form of litigation);
10. Appeal accepted by appellate courts (not all are accepted);
11. Judge who hears appeal writes a published option (which happens with less than 10% of appeals heard).

Clearly, published appellate opinions offer a rarefied window into law-as-practice, where client goals are mostly hidden, and the full array of facts presented at a trial are digested into tiny summaries. Without the careful assistance of a teacher, students are likely to overlook the primacy of client needs and goals.

Client goals are messy and complicated. Learning primarily from appellate opinions and short hypothetical problems reinforces the erroneous view that client goals are unitary and tidy. Most lawyers and judges understand this concept—but most new lawyers have to unlearn false assumptions. One professor reported that, when holding discussions with prominent lawyers and judges in the Berkeley, California, area, she was surprised that the three most prominent perceived gaps in legal education were client-related, but not in the specific way she had thought:

1. Students had not learned how complex and "messy" client stories and desired outcomes were;
2. Students had not learned that broad historical and societal forces affect lawyer roles and the ability of lawyers to help clients achieve their goals; and
3. Students had not learned that, in addition to sharp analysis of legal theories, students need to learn judgment regarding which theories to pursue to assist clients in their stated goals.[3]

To lawyers, these observations are obvious. But somehow, core law school classes miss that the starting point for every case is a client.

---

3. Kristen Holmquist, *Challenging Carnegie*, 61 J. LEGAL EDUC. 353–354 (2012) (citations omitted).

Professor Prompts:

- How can you help your students understand how client goals influence every choice a lawyer makes?
- How can you demonstrate the connection between rules of law articulated by judges in appellate opinions and client needs that were communicated to a lawyer?

The easiest way to incorporate client perspective in a doctrinal class is to ask students to identify client needs and goals in the appellate cases they study.

Professor Prompts:

How can you bring a client perspective into appellate cases you cover in your class? One way is to modify the traditional approach to briefing a case. Rather than focusing narrowly on rule-of-law issues, what else can you ask students to include in a case brief? Have you considered asking them to think about some of the following?

- Who are the parties?
- What happened to them?
- What relief are they seeking?
- Why are they seeking that relief?
- Is there anything about the context of the events (e.g., when did it happen, where did it happen, what was going on in the world at that time?) that would illuminate why the court chose to weigh in on this issue in the way that it did?
- What choices or strategies did the lawyers make in this case? What choices or strategies might they have chosen instead? In what way might client choices have affected choices the lawyers made?

Another way to help students understand the importance of clients is to put students in role as clients. Even very short simulated exercises where students are given roles (e.g., a person negotiating a contract, a person who owns real estate, a person who has been in an accident) can help students understand the primacy of client interests in the law. Even short exercises can include information about client goals, both legal and non-legal, that must be taken into account.

Longer exercises can be developed that require students to apply legal doctrine to help clients solve problems. Instead of using only short problems or hypotheticals, professors can sometimes offer lengthier problems that incorporate more complicated client needs. Lawyers know that legal analysis, by itself, never solves a client problem. Clients have lives (personal and work-related) that produce factors that affect the choices they make. Not all clients are individuals—some are organizations, some are businesses, some are governmental entities. Starting in the first semester of law school, students should be introduced to solving problems based on complex goals. Even in large classes, students can work in small groups and apply rules of law to answer the questions of a realistic simulated client. Realistic client scenarios can form the background for exercises as short as 20–30 minutes or can form the background for exercises that recur throughout a course. When students are put in role to solve problems, they form the understanding that legal analysis usually serves the purpose of helping specific clients with specific problems.

Professors should help students understand that client needs and goals often change as new information about the law and the facts is discovered. When designing realistic client scenarios, professors should help students formulate questions they would want the client to answer—questions about facts, but also questions about goals and choices.

Professor Prompts:

- Are students studying a rule of law, a test, a set of factors, or a policy that can be applied to help solve a client problem?
- Can you develop a client scenario that offers a more fully realized client, one with multiple goals and needs, so that students can develop problem-solving strategies that will incorporate the needs of the client?

Professors may find the chart below helpful in framing the issues that might arise at different stages of a client's case.

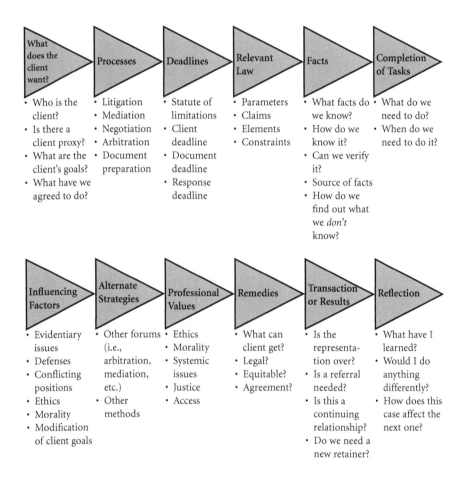

What does the client want?
- Who is the client?
- Is there a client proxy?
- What are the client's goals?
- What have we agreed to do?

Processes
- Litigation
- Mediation
- Negotiation
- Arbitration
- Document preparation

Deadlines
- Statute of limitations
- Client deadline
- Document deadline
- Response deadline

Relevant Law
- Parameters
- Claims
- Elements
- Constraints

Facts
- What facts do we know?
- How do we know it?
- Can we verify it?
- Source of facts
- How do we find out what we *don't* know?

Completion of Tasks
- What do we need to do?
- When do we need to do it?

Influencing Factors
- Evidentiary issues
- Defenses
- Conflicting positions
- Ethics
- Morality
- Modification of client goals

Alternate Strategies
- Other forums (i.e., arbitration, mediation, etc.)
- Other methods

Professional Values
- Ethics
- Morality
- Systemic issues
- Justice
- Access

Remedies
- What can client get?
- Legal?
- Equitable?
- Agreement?

Transaction or Results
- Is the representation over?
- Is a referral needed?
- Is this a continuing relationship?
- Do we need a new retainer?

Reflection
- What have I learned?
- Would I do anything differently?
- How does this case affect the next one?

Professor Prompts:

Consider one class:

- Can you frame the information to be covered from the perspective of one of the categories in the illustration above?
- Can you do so in a way that will help students understand how clients' problems might appear messy to an attorney?
- Can you do so in a way that will show students that clients' cases are rarely as linear as an appellate court opinion might suggest?
- Can you do so in a way that weaves doctrine into the facts the client brings?

Finally, clients and their attorneys often come from different backgrounds. These differences can affect how lawyers help clients. Professors should be sensitive to issues of difference when discussing and creating client exercises. Differences might include gender, race, ethnicity, religion, sexual orientation, income level, educational background, experience with a certain industry or vocation, language, and other factors. Whether to incorporate specific identity issues into a client problem is part of the judgment a professor must exercise when crafting the exercises.

For ideas about how to approach culture in the classroom, please consider visiting *Five Habits of Cross-Cultural Lawyering and More* at http://fivehabitsand more.law.yale.edu.

Chapter 4 Workbook

Fully Understanding the Client's Problem

Course: _____

A. Work for the Professor

Client goals are messy and complicated.

Professor Prompts:

Consider one class:

- Can you frame the information to be covered from the perspective of one of the categories on the illustration on the next page?
- Can you do so in a way that will help students understand how clients' problems might appear messy to an attorney?
- Can you do so in a way that it will show students that clients' cases are rarely as linear as an appellate court opinion might suggest?
- Can you do so in a way that weaves doctrine into the facts the client brings?

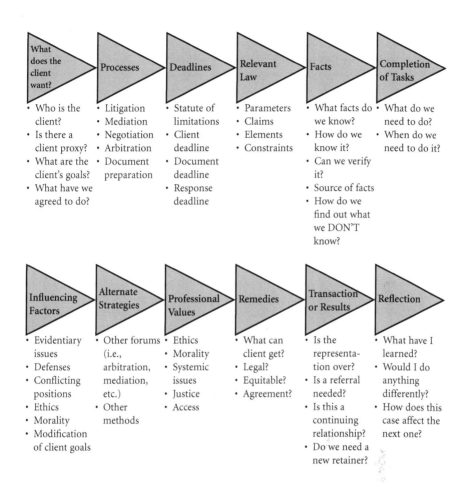

What does the client want?
- Who is the client?
- Is there a client proxy?
- What are the client's goals?
- What have we agreed to do?

Processes
- Litigation
- Mediation
- Negotiation
- Arbitration
- Document preparation

Deadlines
- Statute of limitations
- Client deadline
- Document deadline
- Response deadline

Relevant Law
- Parameters
- Claims
- Elements
- Constraints

Facts
- What facts do we know?
- How do we know it?
- Can we verify it?
- Source of facts
- How do we find out what we DON'T know?

Completion of Tasks
- What do we need to do?
- When do we need to do it?

Influencing Factors
- Evidentiary issues
- Defenses
- Conflicting positions
- Ethics
- Morality
- Modification of client goals

Alternate Strategies
- Other forums (i.e., arbitration, mediation, etc.)
- Other methods

Professional Values
- Ethics
- Morality
- Systemic issues
- Justice
- Access

Remedies
- What can client get?
- Legal?
- Equitable?
- Agreement?

Transaction or Results
- Is the representation over?
- Is a referral needed?
- Is this a continuing relationship?
- Do we need a new retainer?

Reflection
- What have I learned?
- Would I do anything differently?
- How does this case affect the next one?

B. Work for Students

Students need to understand that client goals drive the arguments and strategies lawyers pursue. Client goals are usually multi-layered.

Connecting the classroom to client goals:

Classroom topic	How client goals can be connected to the topic

Appellate case connection to client goals:

Who are the parties? Are they individuals, entities, or representatives?	
What are the parties asking for?	
What happened to the parties?	
What is the context of the case in the larger world? What year is it? What jurisdiction? What is motivating the court to weigh in on this issue?	
What choices or strategies did the lawyer make in this case? What choices or strategies might the lawyer have chosen instead? How might client choices have affected the lawyer's choices or strategies?	
Are there any ethical issues in this case, especially as relate to the attorney-client relationship?	

Students in role as clients:

How might students better understand this week's material if I put them in role as client?	
If the students are in role as client, have I built in several client goals? Client goals might include outcome goals, resource goals, relationship goals, etc.	
How will client goals affect students' understanding of this week's material?	
Is there an educational benefit to giving the client a specific identity (e.g., race, ethnicity, gender, religion, language, etc.) in this exercise?	

Students in role as lawyers formulating client goals:

Is there legal doctrine in this class where a range of client goals has a noticeable impact on choices or strategies the lawyer might pursue?	
Can I create a role-play where the student playing the attorney finds out what the client's major goals are, and the student playing the client is given a rich set of goals?	
Is there an educational benefit to giving the client a specific identity (e.g., race, ethnicity, gender, religion, language, etc.) in this exercise?	

Students in role as lawyers—formulating advice:

Is there a rule of law or legal analysis I am teaching that would benefit from a 20–30 minute in-class exercise where I can provide students with a set of client goals and ask students to advise the client?	
Do I want a self-contained exercise, or do I want to build from a client-interviewing exercise I used earlier in the course? What are the advantages and disadvantages of using the same or a different set of facts?	
Do I want to provide students with a set of options, ask students to generate their own options, or a combination of the two?	
Is this an in-class exercise or an out-of-class exercise? Have I provided students with sufficient guidance on what law to apply (e.g., law from certain pages of the reading assignment, or attachments of law to read, understand, and analyze), or am I expecting students to research the law in a particular jurisdiction?	
Can students reasonably accomplish what I am asking in the given amount of time? Is the amount of time students will spend on this assignment consistent with the educational value in the context of this course?	
What form will the client counseling take? Will it be oral? Written? Letter? Memo?	

Chapter 5

Identifying the Law Needed to Resolve the Problem

For obvious reasons, a law school course is organized around the subject-matter area that is being covered. Subtopics are organized under major topics, and the topics are covered in a logical order. There has probably never been a professor who had so much extra class time that she could add more to this list of major topics, much less to add material that is covered in other courses. Accordingly, students see each area of law as a silo, with each silo filled with the topics presented in the classroom and labeled with the name of the course.

Professors can help their students see the topic they are covering in a larger perspective. They could offer this perspective in a number of ways, none of which takes much class time. However, doing so could make the difference between effectively placing a map in your students' hands and helping them understand the terrain, or sending them out the door not even realizing they will need a map to pass the bar and practice law.

A. Locate the Material within a Larger Context

An easy thing professors could do to help their students understand the larger perspective of the law is to locate their course within larger legal divisions. While this information may seem very basic to professors, for students trying to get their bearing, it is no different than establishing a "you are here" sticker, like on the map at the local mall. It is so much easier to get your bearings and know which way to go when you understand where you are starting from, that there are many different types of stores available, and where the stores are located with respect to each other.

Divisions:

Civil law	⟷	Criminal law
Statutory law	⟷	Common law
Statutory law	⟷	Administrative law
Legal issue	⟷	Ethical issue
Federal law	⟷	State law
Constitutional law	⟷	Federal or state law

In any single course, several divisions could apply, depending on what is covered during a class period. Nothing prevents a professor from using a road map to orient students, and it would seem that lots of road maps would be better than none or a few. If students understand how they reached the silo that is the material in your class, they are more likely to be able to find their way back to that silo after understanding a client's fact pattern.

> **Professor Prompts:**
>
> Consider how your course would appear to a practitioner. Thinking both about the course in general and individual topics more specifically, consider the following:

Does it always appear in a civil or a criminal context?	• Can you make the significance of this distinction clear to your students? • How? • In how many ways?
Is your course driven by statutory law or common law?	• Is there a reason why it is primarily statutory or common law? • Will that reason help students understand the law? • How can you make that distinction and its impact clear to students?
Are the rules found primarily in statutes or in administrative provisions?	• What are the practical implications of where the substantive portions of the law can be found? • Do administrative rules carry less (or more) weight than statutory rules?
Do ethical issues regularly appear?	• Are ethical rules built into the substantive area, or are they found in the rules of professional responsibility? • What are the consequences of violating an ethical rule?
Is the course built on federal law or state law?	• Why are the rules federal rules? • Do the states have their own version of the rules in this area? • If so, will state rules be addressed? • Why or why not?
Do any areas of the course involve constitutional issues?	• How are constitutional issues different from statutory issues? • Which are harder for a practitioner? • Why? • How can you explain this difference to students?

Assessment Suggestions: Periodically throughout the term, have students identify where a case, material, issue, etc. is located within the larger context of the law. The assessment can be as simple as checking the appropriate box or boxes.

Location in the Law	√
Civil law	
Criminal law	
Statutory law	
Common law	
Administrative law	
Ethical issues	
Federal law	
State law	
Constitutional law	

B. Take Advantage of Ground Already Covered

Most courses are cumulative. Concepts that are covered earlier in the term appear later in the term, but as the foundation for new concepts or issues. In the race to cover the cases, most professors gloss over the concepts covered earlier to address the new concepts. However, these areas provide a great opportunity for students to see how the law in a particular subject-matter area is layered and, maybe more importantly, when one issue needs to be resolved in their client's favor before the next issue can be considered. In other words, professors can be aware of when they are interleaving, or mixing material already studied with new material.

Professor Prompts:

Consider your course:

- Can you identify concepts presented early in the term that provide the foundation for a later, perhaps more complex, concept?
- Must the earlier issue be resolved in a client's favor before later concepts can be applied?
- Does the earlier issue become a factor in a later issue?
- Are there issues that often appear together? Why are they covered at different times during the term?
- What do you do to help students understand that the concepts or issues are layered?
- Are students aware of interleaving of the material (mixing the material already studied with new material)?

Alternative Approaches to Covering a Case: Identify a case that has issues that are covered at different times during the term. Rather than approaching a case using IRAC, do not assign the case to your students. Rather, provide students a summary of the facts (whether constructed from the opinion, briefs, etc.) as if presented by a new client requesting assistance. Ask students to identify all the issues they would have to address, including:

- How many issues are present?
- If more than one issue is identified, must a particular issue be resolved in the client's favor before any other issues can be considered?
- Did the client provide all the facts necessary to resolve the issues?
- If not, what additional facts are needed?
- What is the likelihood that the client will be successful on each issue identified? Explain.

After discussing responses to these questions, students can be assigned the case. They can self-assess how well they would have performed for their client.

C. Eliminate the Illusion That the Law Exists in Silos

Professors can destroy the illusion that the law exists in silos. While there is a sound logic for why courses are presented based on topics, such as torts, contracts, constitutional law, etc., this presentation method fails to inform students that, in reality and practice, certain topics transcend courses. It almost feels like an accident if students are presented with a constitutional issue in a tax course, an evidentiary issue in a wills course, or a property issue in a contracts course. This failure to see the rules in their many subject-matter areas hamstrings students when they begin the practice of law. Sitting at their law firm desks, they may be wondering:

- Do collateral damages appear in torts, in contracts, or in both?
- Does what type of legal entity a business operates as impact how it is taxed for federal purposes?
- What evidentiary rules are relevant when trying to establish the decedent's intent when he drafted his will?
- Is there a problem with my taking on this case when the firm, long ago, helped the potential defendant form his LLC?

Because he is not sitting in a particular class when the client walks in the door, the practitioner cannot flip through the material assigned for that class for ideas on how to solve the problem. The client's issue could be one issue from one course, one issue that occurred in multiple courses, several issues that arose in different courses, or an issue for which the law does not provide a remedy, regardless of which course is considered.

Professor Prompts:

1. Does a topic you are covering arise in another course?
2. How can you make your students aware of its application in other courses?
3. Are there differences in how it is applied in other courses?
4. Would understanding those differences help your students understand how it applies in your course?

Assessment Suggestions: If a case addresses a concept that students learned in another course, require students to:

1. Draft a short summary of the law as covered in the other course.
2. Draft a short summary of the law as covered in your course.
3. Explain any differences and similarities in application.

D. Be Clear about Which Courses Provide a Supporting Role

The professor can help orient students by recognizing which courses are in a supporting role. While they are legitimate courses in themselves, these topics rarely come up unless there is an issue that arises from another area. Prime examples are evidence, administrative law, and ethics. Professors in these areas can provide a huge benefit to students by placing the rules well within the subject-matter context whenever possible. Similarly, professors who teach a subject-matter area where evidentiary rules may apply or administrative rules are relevant or ethical issues regularly appear can make the connection between the topic being studied and the supporting-role course.

Professor Prompts:

With respect to your course:

1. In what areas do evidentiary issues arise?
2. In what areas do administrative rules apply?
3. In what areas do ethical considerations arise?

Alternative Approach to Covering a Case: Rather than approaching a case using IRAC, do not assign the case to your students. Instead provide students a summary of the facts (whether constructed from the opinion, briefs, etc.) as if presented by a new client requesting assistance. Ask students to identify all the issues they would have to address, including:

- Any substantive issues.
- Any evidentiary / administrative / ethical issues.
- How they would approach the evidentiary / administrative / ethical issues.
- How important the evidentiary / administrative / ethical issues are to success for the client.
- How they would approach resolving the evidentiary / administrative / ethical issues.

After discussing responses to these questions, students can be assigned the case. They can self-assess how well they would have performed for their client.

E. Legal Triage

When graduates begin practicing law, if they are in private practice, they will need to be able to discern whether clients' issues are within the graduates' area of practice. This determination might happen when the client walks in the door and asks to speak to a lawyer. Or it might happen electronically. Most law firms have a webpage that provides information about the firm. It also provides a means by which potential clients can contact the firm about representation. Whether potential clients are screened in person or via the website, someone must determine whether practitioners can assist potential clients. Students can begin thinking about the larger context of the law by beginning to think about this legal triage process.

Assessment Suggestions: Have students respond to the following:

- What types of clients do you expect to represent?
- In what areas do you expect to practice?

Draft three to five questions that could be asked to a potential client, whether through a website or in person, to determine:

- The topic area(s) presented by the potential client's facts;
- Whether the law provides a remedy; and
- Whether you or your firm may be interested in representing the potential client.

Chapter 5 Workbook

Identifying the Law Needed to Resolve the Problem

Course: _____

A. Work for the Professor

An easy thing professors could do to help students understand the larger perspective of the law is to locate their course within larger legal divisions. While this information may seem very basic to professors, for students trying to get their bearings, it is no different than establishing a "you are here" sticker, like on the map at the local mall. It is so much easier to get your bearings and know which way to go when you understand where you are starting from, that there are many different types of stores available, and where the stores are located in relation to each other.

> **Professor Prompts:**
>
> Consider how your course would appear to a practitioner. Thinking both about the course in general and the topics more specifically, consider the following:

Does it always appear in a civil or a criminal context?	• Can you make the significance of this distinction clear to your students? • How? • In how many ways?	
Is your course driven by statutory law or common law?	• Is there a reason why it is primarily statutory or common law? • Will that reason help students understand the law? • How can you make that distinction and its impact clear to students?	
Are the rules found primarily in statutes or in administrative provisions?	• What are the practical implications of where the substantive portions of the law can be found? • Do administrative rules carry less (or more) weight than statutory rules?	
Do ethical issues regularly appear?	• Are ethical rules built in to the substantive area or are they found in the rules of professional responsibility? • What are the consequences of violating an ethical rule?	
Is the course built on federal law or state law?	• If federal, why are the rules federal rules? • Do the states have their own version of the rules in this area? • If so, will state rules be addressed? • Why or why not?	
Do any areas of the course involve constitutional issues?	• How are constitutional issues different from statutory issues? • Which are harder for a practitioner? • Why? • How can you explain this difference to students?	

Most courses are cumulative. Because of time constraints, most professors gloss over the concepts covered earlier to address the new concepts. However, these areas provide a great opportunity for students to see how the law in a particular subject-matter area is layered and, maybe more importantly, when one issue needs to be resolved in their client's favor before the next issue can be considered. Professors can work with recurring themes in their courses to help students understand how the law is layered.

Consider your course:

Can you identify concepts presented early in the term that provide the foundation for a later, perhaps more complex, concept?	
Must the earlier issue be resolved in a client's favor before later concepts can be applied?	
Does the earlier issue become a factor in a later issue?	
Are there issues that often appear together? Why are they covered at different times during the term?	
What do you do to help students understand that the concepts or issues are layered?	
Are students aware of interleaving of material (mixing the material already studied with new material)?	

While there is a sound logic for why courses are presented based on topics, the problem with this presentation method is that it fails to show students that, in reality and practice, certain topics transcend courses. It almost feels like an accident when students are presented with a constitutional issue in a tax course, an evidentiary issue in a wills course, or a property issue in a contracts course. This failure to see the rules in their many subject-matter areas hamstrings students when they begin practicing law. Professors should destroy the illusion that the law exists in silos.

Does a topic you are covering arise in another course?	
How can you make your students aware of its application in other courses?	
Are there differences in how it is applied in other courses?	
Would understanding those differences help your students understand how it applies in your course?	

Professors can help orient students by recognizing which courses are in a supporting role and which courses have issues that are addressed in classes that play a supporting role.

In what areas do evidentiary issues arise?	
In what areas do administrative rules apply?	
In what areas do ethical considerations arise?	
In what other areas do issues arise that are not directly covered in your course?	

B. Assessments for Students

Students should understand the larger perspective of the law and how the course is located within larger legal divisions. Ask students to demonstrate that they understand the larger perspective of the law and how the course material is located within larger legal divisions.

Periodically throughout the term, have students identify where a case, material, issue, etc. is located within the larger context of the law. The assessment can be as simple as checking the appropriate box or boxes.

Location in the Law	√
Civil law	
Criminal law	
Statutory law	
Common law	
Administrative law	
Ethical issues	
Federal law	
State law	
Constitutional law	

All areas of law have parts where the issues are layered. Often, one issue needs to be resolved in the client's favor before the next issue can be considered. Take advantage of ground already covered in your course by helping students see how the law in a particular subject-matter area is layered and, maybe more importantly, when one issue needs to be resolved in the client's favor before the next issue can be considered. Have students demonstrate that they can address layered issues.

Alternative Approach to Covering a Case: Identify a case that has issues that are covered at different times during the term. Rather than approaching a case using IRAC, do not assign the case to your students. Rather, provide students a summary of the facts (whether constructed from the opinion, briefs, etc.) as if presented by a new client requesting assistance. Ask students to identify all the issues they would have to address, including:

- How many issues are present?
- If more than one issue is identified, must a particular issue be resolved in the client's favor before any other issues can be considered?
- Did the client provide all the facts necessary to resolve the issues?
- If not, what additional facts are needed?
- What is the likelihood that the client will be successful on each issue identified? Explain.

After discussing responses to these questions, students can be assigned the case. They can self-assess how well they would have performed for their client.

Failing to see that the law does *not* exist in silos can hamstrings graduates when they begin practicing law. The professor can destroy the illusion by helping students better understand how issues are interwoven among law school courses. Expect students to connect the silos.

Assessment Suggestions: If a case addresses a concept that students learned in another course, require students to:

1. Draft a short summary of the law as covered in the other course.
2. Draft a short summary of the law as covered in your course.
3. Explain any differences and similarities in application.

Professors can help orient students by recognizing which courses are in a supporting role and which courses have issues that are addressed in classes that play a supporting role. Create situations that allow students to see issues addressed in supporting courses and how issues in supporting courses arise in the subject-matter area.

Alternative Approach to Covering a Case: Rather than approaching a case using IRAC, do not assign the case to your students. Rather, provide students a summary of the facts (whether constructed from the opinion, briefs, etc.) as if presented by a new client requesting assistance. Ask students to identify all the issues they would have to address, including:

- Any substantive issues.
- Any evidentiary / administrative / ethical issues.
- How they would approach the evidentiary / administrative / ethical issues.
- How important the evidentiary / administrative / ethical issue is to success for the client.
- How they would approach resolving the evidentiary / administrative / ethical issue.

After discussing responses to these questions, students can be assigned the case. They can self-assess how well they would have performed for their client.

Students should be challenged to begin thinking about the law more holistically. They can do this by trying legal triage.

Assessment Suggestions: Have students respond to the following:

- What types of clients do you expect to represent?
- In what areas do you expect to practice?

Draft three to five questions that could be asked to a potential client, whether through a website or in person, to determine:

- the topic area(s) presented by the potential client's facts;
- whether the law provides a remedy; and
- whether you or your firm may be interested in representing the potential client.

Chapter 6

Processing Systems: Retrieving Legal Rules to Envision Possible Outcomes

When helping clients, lawyers go through mental checklists to find possible solutions. Typically, these checklists start with identifying rules of law that might apply. But what is a rule of law? And how do we teach students to find the right rules to begin the analysis?

At the beginning of law school, students are taught to identify the "rule" to apply to an issue. Most new law students, a few weeks into their first set of courses, can isolate rules of law that are clearly stated in appellate cases and have a basic understanding of what those rules mean. In part, this is because the entire structure of an appellate case is designed to lead to a recitation of a rule of law. Merely citing and even understanding that rule as expressed in that case is, of course, a woefully incomplete understanding of what the rule means in the broader context of its subject matter, fact variations, client goals, and society.

Lawyers understand that rules of law are practically useless if the lawyers cannot find the right ones when they need them. Engaging in legal analysis in the daily life of a lawyer means having mental structures to draw upon when searching for legal rules that will be used to solve problems. Legal problems come in the form of facts first, and lawyers use those facts to trigger rules of law that they have learned.

Skill-building in the early law school curriculum involves primarily teaching students how to build mental structures that they can retrieve later. These structures are taught in the context of a body of doctrine that is thought to be foundational. It is essential that students understand a variety of foundational tools for setting up these structures. These tools include:

- Elements;
- Standards and tests;
- Factors;
- Sequencing;
- Flexible thinking; and
- Normative values.

A good student will understand the differences among these tools, and will call upon the proper tools when analyzing a legal problem. A good professor will explicitly identify these tools, teach students how to use them, require students to actually use them, and assess whether and how well students do use them.

Professor Prompts:

- When you talk about a "rule of law," is it clear what kind of rule you mean?
- Do students understand that there are different types of legal rules?

A. Elements

Perhaps the easiest tools are legal elements. As their name suggests, elements are essential components of some causes of action and crimes. Unlike "factors" and "tests," elements are a check-off-the-list set of factual conditions, all of which must be present for the cause of action or crime to succeed. The person seeking relief (normally a plaintiff in a civil case or a prosecutor in a criminal case) must carry the burden of proving that each element is met. Likewise, a defendant carries the burden of proving elements of an affirmative defense. The critical understanding of elements is that each one must be proved, or the entire cause of action fails.

Elements are usually memorized as sets, and they generally come in sets of 3–7. Thus, they are easily assessed by short-answer quizzes, flash cards, or other rote memorization tools. Just as doctors memorize symptoms to create a mental bank for processing facts, lawyers memorize elements for the same reason. Appellate cases, the backbone of most first-year law casebooks, consist primarily of borderline scenarios, where it can be argued either way — that an element exists or does not. But most factual clusters that appear in real life contain clearer evidence of the presence or absence of elements. As a consequence, students sometimes miss that when an element is clearly missing, the entire cause of action fails. Likewise, when all elements are clearly met, the cause of action will succeed, absent credibility problems. In that sense, elements create a zero-sum game: they are there, or they are not, and one side either wins or loses.

How elements are defined, however, may be more ambiguous. Most students understand the concept of elements, but don't see that sometimes factual interpretation can lead to arguments both for and against the establishment of an element. Conversely, students sometimes fail to see that an element might be clearly defined and unambiguous. Winnowing ambiguous from unambiguous elements is a skill learned by a new lawyer, and is usually the first step when imagining possible outcomes for a legal problem.

For example, an element might require that the defendant be a resident of X state. If the defendant is an individual who has only one clear residence located in a specific state, it will be easy to establish (or show that one cannot establish) that element. But if the defendant is an out-of-state corporation, "residency" might be harder to establish. When an element is subject to factual interpretation, there is often a "test" or a "standard" involved that contains sufficient ambiguity that might make it unclear what the answer is.

It is important that students understand that not every element is subject to a standard or test. When one is, it is far more likely to be assessed on an exam because it will require using the skill of legal analysis.

Bottom line: when a client presents with a legal problem, quickly looking for elements is the first step in understanding possible outcomes to assist that client.

B. Standards and Tests

What is the difference between a "standard" and a "test"? A standard is a conclusory label used to identify a method for determining whether a set of facts meets a test. Examples of legal standards are "objective," "subjective," "reasonable person," "with knowledge," "reckless," and "community."

A test is usually a series of questions designed to determine whether a standard is met. Sometimes a test requires that all of the parts are answered a certain way, and sometimes a test allows for balancing the answers. When the test requires that all parts be met, it becomes like a set of mini-elements, but ones that are designed to determine whether a larger element is present. Usually such tests can be taught as "x number of questions" that always accompany a particular element. For example, consequential damages in contracts must always meet a two-part test. Sometimes, a part of the test may be subject to a further test. When a test does not require that all parts be met, but instead balancing is involved, the questions are usually called "factors." Factors are discussed below. The best way to assess "tests" is through application. Fact-driven problems are good ways to assess "tests," because they provide more room for offering different interpretations of the same set of facts.

To re-cap: elements, which are required components of a cause of action, can be memorized as lists. When a set of facts contains elements of a cause of action, students will begin to compare the facts with a list of elements. Most elements are either present or absent. But some elements are ambiguous and subject to legal tests or standards. Legal tests or standards are often subject to interpretation and thus those elements are less likely to be clearly present or absent, so they are often capable of argument by both sides.

When teaching elements, the professor should help students identify which elements are typically clearly present or absent, and which elements are subject to standards or tests. In the classroom, students should be encouraged to identify facts that support opposite conclusions about whether a test is met. Appellate cases often contain facts that help each side of the argument. Students can be divided into groups to identify facts that help the plaintiff and facts that help the defendant. Problems can be introduced that are designed to require students to argue both sides of legal standards and tests, but they should be tailored so that students can see that sometimes the standards and tests are clearly met or unmet, while at other times the result is more ambiguous.

Asking students to color-code problems is a good way to assess whether they understand the differences between elements, standards, rules, and tests.

Bottom line: When a lawyer needs to use a standard or a test to evaluate whether an element can be established, deeper factual inquiry is usually required. Greater ambiguity is introduced, and whether a litigation outcome is possible becomes less clear.

Professor Prompts:

- Do students know that elements must all be met for a cause of action to succeed?
- Do they know that many elements are easy either to establish or to show that they are not established?
- Have you helped students to see which elements are more likely to be arguable?

C. Factors

When the law requires a balancing of policies to determine a rule of law, the policies are typically called "factors." Factors are a set of questions that usually convey the idea of a continuum, one where the weight of a set of factors shifts the answer one way or the other. Constitutional law is full of balancing tests, which are sets of factors to be weighed, as are equitable causes of action. Not all factors are equally considered, however; some are more important than others. The main idea that students need to know is that factors are more flexible than elements or tests. There is more discretion, and usually the ideas are more related to policy. In this way, factors often call upon the flexible thinking and normative value tools, discussed below. Thus, for factors, it is almost always possible to argue more than one side.

The weighing of factors should almost always be done in context. Assessments must be fact-sensitive and require students to apply the factors to specific factual contexts.

Bottom line: Factors introduce the opportunity for lawyers to consider policy when understanding available outcomes.

D. Sequencing

Another key idea for processing legal rules has to do with sequencing. Lawyers only ask certain questions if other questions are answered a certain way. Students who analyze issues out of sequence seem disorganized and lacking in some basic understanding of a subject. Each subject matter has its own internal logic and sequence, and the professor needs to show students how to follow that order.

Sequencing is an issue of efficiency. It would be a waste of time and money for a lawyer to spend time researching and analyzing issues that are irrelevant because pre-conditions do not exist. For example, it is premature to discuss proximate cause if there is no duty in negligence. Duty is harder to prove, and without it, none of the other elements of negligence matter. In this way, we might call "duty" a "threshold" issue. Similarly, an attorney would never perform extensive analyses of consequential damages if direct damages could not be proven: without direct damages, consequential damages cannot be had.

Professors can help students understand sequencing in several ways. Concept maps and flow charts are excellent tools for showing sequencing. Both offer visual tools for mapping the order of questions that must be asked. Call and response in the classroom is another good technique for drilling sequence.

When presenting the class with a fact scenario, professors can ask, "What is the first question?" After writing that on the board, they can then say, "What comes next?" And so on. By the third or fourth problem, most students are adept at knowing the order of the questions for tackling a particular type of problem.

Finally, students' outlines should drive home sequence and order, especially after students have learned a chunk of material. Requiring students to create an outline, either alone or in groups, is a good way to assess whether they have understood a section of the course.

Some analyses are more prone to sequence than others. Some elements, parts, or factors are equally situated in the sequence, while others are strictly pre-conditions, and still others are merely inefficient if discussed prematurely. Students who can tell when sequencing matters will produce more efficient, tighter analysis than the ones who cannot.

Bottom line: Lawyers who understand sequencing will spend less time chasing irrelevant information. Good sequencing will make possible outcomes clearer, sooner.

E. Flexible Thinking

The common law system is built on the creative tension between a preference for the use of objective rules and the need to reinvent rules when conditions change. The idea is to apply the same rules to the same facts, but with humans, the facts are almost never precisely the same. Part of the lawyer's job is to advocate for creative change in light of new facts. New facts can be experiences that are different, or they can be the same experiences in a different cultural milieu. Of all of the tools for processing legal rules, flexible thinking, sometimes called elastic thinking, is one of the most difficult for students. Memorizing a rule is easy compared to the daunting task of imagining a different rule in light of changed conditions. And some students see flexible thinking as abdicating the rule of law, rather than a natural part of its fabric. Professors must help students understand the importance of flexible thinking, especially in a time when change is occurring faster and faster.

What does flexible thinking entail? At its core, it is a method for imagining different possibilities—different legal rules, different factual settings, different outcomes—when the traditional models cannot solve the problem. Many factors have converged to make this a time when flexible thinking is especially important.

They include:

- Advances in technology;
- Transformations in how, where, and with whom people work;
- Commingling of ethnicities and cultures;
- Shifts in demographics (e.g., rural to urban, younger to older, religious to agnostic, etc.);
- Reconstructions of power dynamics (e.g., between genders, races, sexual identities, etc.); and
- Metamorphoses in core values.

These factors affect how we think about the law as a problem-solving mechanism, and they often call for creative shifts in legal rules and processes. Every case that professors teach students is a rich tapestry of relationships that reflect certain understandings of how the world works. In a world characterized by change, flexible thinking is necessary.

For example, specialists in ethics have had to adapt rules of confidentiality to a world where information can inadvertently be published to the world on the internet. Divorce lawyers have had to adapt to the increase in inter-cultural marriages (and consequent divorces) when fashioning rules of fairness in custody, spousal support, and property division. Many students find it especially difficult to understand that cases are always decided in the context of a time, place, and culture, and that common law is built on the necessity of flexible thinking.

Methods for generating flexible thinking among students might include:

- Discussing appellate cases to make explicit the context of the time and era the case was decided (e.g., why might courts have been leery of contracts involving "conjuring spirits" in the late 19th and early 20th centuries?).
- Brainstorming different ways to frame legal issues. If the legal issue is seen one way, one set of rules apply; framed differently, a different set of rules might apply. The careful lawyer intentionally tests different ways to see legal issues.
- Questioning assumptions about the facts. Each of us applies cognitive schemas based on our own experiences that fill in gaps in information; therefore, consciously learning to question one's own assumptions is a critical skill in flexible thinking.
- Critically examining one's conclusions. Intentional efforts to play "devil's advocate" against one's own strongly held views can produce a shift in perception of the problem and possible solutions to it.

In the classroom, flexible thinking can be promoted in several ways. The paradigmatic Socratic method is one way to push students into flexible thinking.

Posing a set of differing hypotheticals, and requiring students to respond by applying rules of law and analysis, is a good start. Small groups can be used to promote flexible thinking. Groups can be given slightly different parameters on a common set of facts, with reporting back to the larger groups so that differences can be analyzed. Brainstorming alternative "fact theories" can help students imagine how variations in context affects choice of rules and analysis. Appellate cases can be dissected for their cultural and relationship assumptions, with attention paid to how a similar setting today might or might not merit a different rule, analysis, or result.

A different way flexible thinking arises is when legal actors categorize certain types of cases in certain ways. As the world evolves, lawyers are constantly reviewing whether the categories still make sense, whether the same ideas belong in the same categories, whether new categories are needed, and whether new ideas belong in old categories. For example, Contracts grapples with adequate and sufficient consideration. Do crypto-currencies change the fundamental understanding of either of these concepts in any way? What about reproductive technology, artificial intelligence, or the "dark web"? Do these new ideas affect what we believe should or should not be exchanged for money and whether the arrangement is enforceable in court? When students engage with cases, sometimes over a hundred years old, can professors connect events and ideas that were current in the 19th century to legal categories that were created? Helping students understand the purpose of the categories will help them develop tools to advance arguments about new ideas in the future. This is a form of flexible thinking.

A good way to assess flexible thinking is assigning students to consider a client's goals in light of the creation of a new written product (e.g., contract clauses or an assumption of risk policy). Students can be given a simulated client video or letter, with alternative legal language, and be asked to (1) evaluate the offered language and (2) create language in students' own words. Such an assessment will require students to think about how to accomplish a legal goal in a variety of different ways, while paying attention to current law. This type of assessment uses the highest level of Bloom's Taxonomy, evaluation and creation, and can be engaged in even by first-term students, especially during class and using small groups.

Bottom line: Helping students see the necessity of flexible thinking in the development of the law will help widen the scope of possible outcomes available to clients. Requiring students to practice flexible thinking will help them create multiple potential outcomes.

F. Normative Values

The final tool for processing rules of law is examining normative values in the law. Generally, "normative" means assigning positive value to certain outcomes and negative value to other outcomes. In American law, this means judges, legislators, and executives select certain legal rules because of the value they place on outcomes produced by those rules.

Each legal subject has implicit normative values. Understanding the normative framework for each area of the law is an essential condition for students making creative arguments. Sometimes first-year students are warned, "It doesn't matter whether it is fair, the only thing that matters is whether the rule applies." This is bad advice. It *does* matter whether a rule produces a fair outcome, but legal argument must be clothed in language that rule-makers are trained to see as permissible when arguing fairness. In a common law system, there are multiple parts to arguing fairness:

- First, lawyers must understand why the rule-makers believed that the rule produced good outcomes.
- Next, lawyers should ask whether, under new facts, that good outcome is defeated using the same rule; if so, can lawyers argue for a new variation on the rule under these facts?
- If the same outcome is achieved, lawyers can look to whether society has shifted in its understanding of what a good outcome is. Can they make an argument that the rule is outdated, and a different outcome is desirable?

Merely arguing fairness, without taking the time to understand the normative rules of the doctrine, will rarely, if ever, succeed. In other words, lawyers cannot change normative rules unless they first understand the values embedded in the doctrine. Professors must, therefore, teach students to understand the normative values embedded in the doctrine. Then students need to be taught to ask whether those values are upheld by continuing to use the same rules of law. Finally, students should be encouraged to ask whether new or different values should be substituted.

Discussion threads are a good way to help students navigate the normative values embedded in the doctrine. Professors can ask students to think about such questions as:

- Why do you think the judges created this rule?
- What do you think the result of this rule has been or will be?

- The court says it is wanting X result, but doesn't this rule actually promote Y?
- Do you think this is a good rule? Why or why not?

Likewise, professors in the classroom can help students formulate fairness arguments by probing them to articulate whether the rule promotes the outcome desired by the rule-maker, whether a different rule would better promote that same outcome, or whether the outcome has become undesirable.

Bottom line: When assessing possible outcomes, lawyers should ask whether the current rule application produces a fair result. Lawyers should be able to argue to keep or change a rule based on a well-founded fairness argument.

Chapter 6 Workbook

Processing Systems: Retrieving Legal Rules to Envision Possible Outcomes

When we talk about IRAC, we often mix up different types of "rules of law." How can you help students appreciate the different types of rule statements and application?

Class 1	Elements	Standards & Tests	Factors	Sequencing	Flexible Thinking	Normative Values
When preparing for class, which types of legal rules are in this week's material?						
What types of classroom experiences can I develop to help students practice identifying different types of legal rules / processes involved?						
Have I used this material to connect different types of processes throughout the course?						
In helping students review material, have I differentiated between different types of legal processes?						

Assessment Suggestions: Short-answer quizzes after a class are a great way to assess elements, standards, and tests. You can give the quiz in class, or post it for students to take at the end of class. It does not have to be graded if the students can see the correct answers after they submit their answers.

Short fact problems are a good way to assess standards with tests and factors. If you divide the class into small groups, each group can tackle a slightly different problem using the same standard with tests or factors. Have each group report back to the class, making sure the group identifies all the facts that tend toward one side or the other. Or ask one group to identify facts that support the existence of a standard with tests or factors, and the other group to identify facts that go against the standard or factors being met.

More complex essay-type fact patterns are great for sequencing practice. You can turn an appellate case into a fact pattern and ask students to analyze using the proper sequence. You can lead a series of practice essays in class where the class calls out the proper steps as you work through the problem. You can also have students turn in an outline of material to demonstrate proper sequence analysis.

Flexible thinking can be assessed by asking students to create solutions to problems. Given a certain area of law, ask students to draft an opinion letter, memo to the file, contract clause, or other document. Let students know what the objective is, and ask them to craft innovative language or suggest an innovative solution. Flexible thinking can also be enhanced by giving students a couple of sentences tersely outlining a problem and asking them to brainstorm fact theories. For example, "A man walks into your office and says someone knocked on his door and said she had bought his house. He has no idea who she is or why she thinks she owns his house. List fact theories that might lead to this result that you will want to investigate."

Discussion threads are a terrific way to ask students to engage in normative thinking and also figure out what they do and do not understand. If posted before a class, students can weigh in on "should" questions (e.g., "Should the standard for X be objective or subjective? What are the benefits of either approach?" or "Should there be exceptions to Y rule? Why or why not?"). Reading a discussion thread will tell you a lot about what your students are and are not understanding about the material.

Chapter 7

Formulating Advice

After analyzing options, the next step for a lawyer is formulating advice. If understanding what a client wants is the entrance into most legal problem-solving, answering the question, "What can a client get?" is the value the lawyer adds to the equation. Delivering that information to clients is central to thinking like a lawyer.

Formulating advice involves several steps. First, the lawyer has to understand the client's goals (see Chapter 4). Students should understand that advising a client is based on what the client wants, not based on some assumption of what a person would want. Chapter 4 offers suggestions for helping students see that central premise. Second, the lawyer has to understand the legal process and analysis that will result in possible avenues for solving the client's issues in light of their goals. Chapters 5 and 6 offer suggestions for helping students understand how to use legal analysis to test whether avenues are available to the client. Third, lawyers need to evaluate other factors that might offer a fuller array of options—whether there are mediation or arbitration or settlement options, whether there are witnesses who may not appear, whether there are evidence problems, whether the client has financial constraints, and so on. Formulating advice means that the attorney should suggest an array of options that are possible and practical, and consider and explain the upsides and downsides of the options based on the client's needs and goals.

Students are asked very early in law school to answer questions such as, "If your client asked you whether she had a claim, what would you tell her?" This is a common call of the question on law school exams, even in the first year. Over time, students could logically assume that the only important question a client might have is whether she could make a claim under a particular legal doctrine given a narrow set of facts. But the more important question might be whether the client would want to pursue that claim in the first place.

As discussed in Chapter 4, when students are asked to formulate legal advice, they need to work through scenarios with a richer set of facts. This can be done in short exercises as well as longer ones. Hypothetical simulations can be peppered with factors, such as:

- Whether clients have other things going on in life that influence legal process;
- Whether evidence will be difficult or impossible to come by;
- Whether there are moral, ethical, or ideological issues that affect the decisions clients need to make;
- Whether the opposing party has constraints that affect resolution of the problem;
- Whether something about the decision-maker affects a likely result; and
- Whether time or money or other resources affect how difficult or easy it will be to pursue a lengthy, although possibly successful, course of action.

Students need to learn that sometimes advice is one-sided: that is, not every client's case has even one potentially successful legal avenue. Giving students a problem where there is no close question, no borderline, "maybe" answer, can teach students that sometimes the answers are clear and not always positive. This should lead to a discussion about what other options they might be able to offer a client (e.g., counseling, mediation, adjusting goals, etc.).

Doctrinal classes are not typically the place where students learn specific counseling skills. Law school offers courses designed solely to teach those skills. But examples that help students apply doctrine should be created consistent with realistic, complex factors that typically affect client decision-making, even when used to dissect a very narrow legal doctrine.

> **Professor Prompt:**
>
> When you are teaching a particular legal doctrine, are there opportunities to provide students with scenarios that require them to not only parse the legal elements, standards, policies, or factors, but also require them to grapple with client goals and outside factors?

Chapter 4 discussed the idea that important differences in identity or background of the lawyer and client can affect the attorney-client relationship. Understanding these types of differences can become key aids or impediments in helping a client understand options and make choices. Professor Paul Tremblay recommends a three-part process for discovering how differences in client and lawyer culture might affect client counseling. In his article, *Interviewing and Counseling Across Cultures: Heuristics and Biases,* 9 CLINICAL L. REV. 373 (2002), Professor Tremblay first recommends that lawyers learn basic cultural differences when representing clients from particular, identifiable groups (especially regarding interpersonal space, body language, time and priorities, narrative preferences, and science/religion filters). Second, lawyers must place equal emphasis on taking care *not* to stereotype clients from identifiable groups by assuming that a particular client shares all of the dominant preferences of her or his group. Lawyers must discuss these process issues with clients. Third, Professor Tremblay advises that lawyers understand their own preferences, so that they can realize that their own dominant interactive modes might be the same as or different from their clients'.

Most professors will not choose to spend time on all of these ideas in a doctrinal classroom, but when crafting student exercises or client hypotheticals, or when discussing how to present options to a client, keeping these basic intercultural ideas in mind is important. Intercultural awareness should be a key background idea when crafting client exercises, and it is equally salient when assessing cultural differences that may exist between students in the classroom, or between students and professors. The website *Five Habits of Cross-Cultural Lawyering and More* has many suggestions for class exercises related to cultural awareness. You can find it at http://fivehabitsandmore .law.yale.edu.

As discussed in Chapters 5, 6, and 8, professors should seek opportunities to require students to apply what they are learning, practice legal thinking skills, and create new outcomes for clients. Exercises that require students to formulate legal advice can produce high-level thinking and learning. Such exercises can include:

- Drafting opinion letters based on client information;
- Drafting memos to the client file based on a video of a client interview;
- Drafting tools for teaching a client about the law, such as flowcharts, written outlines, Prezi, or PowerPoint presentations; and
- Counseling simulations.

When asking students to formulate advice, also suggest that students take into account:

- Personal characteristics of the client, if important (e.g., age, ethnicity, race, gender, religious affiliation, etc.);
- If the client is not an individual, but is a corporate entity, non-profit, or the like, how that status affects what and how advice is given; specifically, what are the ethical implications of giving advice to a non-individual entity? and
- The education level of the client (touching upon the idea that using jargon may be inappropriate, depending on the client).

Professor Prompt:

What types of exercises can you ask students to perform that will require them to relate legal doctrine to client goals and outside factors, resulting in students' listing the strengths and weaknesses of a variety of options a client might pursue?

Assessment Suggestions: You can easily assess whether students have understood available legal options in relation to client goals by asking them to:

- Write an opinion letter to a client; be sure to tell them enough about the client so they can write in an appropriate tone, education level, and industry understanding.
- Write a memo to the client file outlining the strengths and weaknesses of various client options, relating those options to client goals and the strength of the legal case. Ask students to list follow-up questions for a client or advise a client in a role play.
- Create a chart or map for a client, explaining options.

Chapter 7 Workbook

Formulating Advice

Course: _____

Students need to understand that client goals drive the arguments and strategies lawyers pursue. Client goals are usually multi-layered.

The following exercises may be done inside or outside of class.

Connecting the classroom to client goals:

Classroom topic	How client goals can be connected to the topic

Appellate case connection to client goals:

Who are the parties? Are they individuals, entities, or representatives?	
What are the parties asking for?	
What happened to the parties?	
What is the context of the case in the larger world? What year is it? What jurisdiction? What is motivating the court to weigh in on this issue?	
What choices or strategies did the lawyer make in this case? What choices or strategies might the lawyer have chosen instead? How might client choices have affected the lawyer's choices or strategies?	
Are there any ethical issues in this case, especially as they relate to the attorney-client relationship?	

Students in role as clients:

How might students better understand this week's material if I put students in role as client?	
If students are in role as client, have I built in several client goals? Client goals might include outcome goals, resource goals, relationship goals, etc.	
How will client goals affect students' understanding of this week's material?	
Is there an educational benefit to giving the client a specific identity (e.g., race, ethnicity, gender, religion, language, etc.) in this exercise?	

Students in role as lawyers formulating client goals:

Is there legal doctrine in this class where a range of client goals has a noticeable impact on choices or strategies the lawyer might pursue?	
Can I create a role-play where the student playing the attorney finds out what the client's major goals are, and the student playing the client is given a rich set of goals?	
Is there an educational benefit to giving the client a specific identity (e.g., race, ethnicity, gender, religion, language, etc.) in this exercise?	

Students in role as lawyers—formulating advice:

Is there a rule of law or legal analysis I am teaching that would benefit from a 20–30 minute in-class exercise where I can provide students with a set of client goals and ask students to advise the client?	
Do I want a self-contained exercise, or do I want to build from a client interviewing exercise I used earlier in the course? What are the advantages and disadvantages of using the same or a different set of facts?	
Do I want to provide students with a set of options, ask students to generate their own options, or a combination of the two?	
Is this an in-class exercise or an out-of-class exercise? Have I provided students with sufficient guidance on what law to apply (e.g., law from certain pages of the reading assignment, or attachments of law to read, understand, and analyze), or am I expecting students to research the law in a particular jurisdiction?	
Can students reasonably accomplish what I am asking in the given amount of time? Is the amount of time students will spend on this assignment consistent with the educational value in the context of this course?	
What form will the client counseling take? Will it be oral? Written? Letter? Memo?	

Chapter 8

Creating New Outcomes: Working toward Creativity

Professors are subject-matter experts, charged with the task of conveying the knowledge that comprises their subject matter to their students. But let's be fair. While professors may state that *understanding* the subject matter is their goal (and they may even have that as a learning outcome), if they take a hard look at these expectations, they really are expecting something more. They want students to be able to understand how the area *works*, to understand how the knowledge can be used to benefit a client.

The professors' expectations can be broken down into (at least) two separate goals: first, learning the content or foundational *information*. For information to become knowledge, students must make meaning of the information. That leads to the second goal: students must acquire *knowledge* of a subject-matter area. At this point, professors should recognize a third goal. Professors want students to *use* that knowledge to effectively engage in problem-solving. That is what lawyers are expected to do: solve the problems that clients bring them. Knowledge that is understood in a way that makes it available to assist with problem-solving is significantly better than information that is merely memorized. In other words, students must be able to *do*, not just *know*. This "doing" is not simply responding to hypotheticals professors use to expound on the material covered during a class. This "doing" is what happens when students begin the practice of law. While most professors focus on the first and second goals, they could be focusing on how to create a learning environment in which students reach the third goal.

> **Professor Prompts:**
>
> - What do practitioners in this area *do*?
> - Can you connect what you are doing in the classroom to what a practitioner actually does?

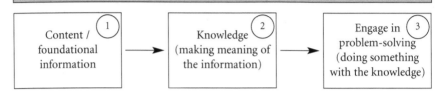

(1) If this were a cooking class, the professor might expect students to be able to identify flour, sugar, eggs, etc. They should understand which ingredients are dry or wet, which have leavening properties, which are bitter or salty, etc. This information will provide the basis from which all cooking will be accomplished. For example, if students do not understand the difference between baking powder and baking soda, they will not understand when a recipe would call for one and not the other.

(2) With that foundational information, students begin to make knowledge: how to beat eggs until they form peaks; how to make a sauce for a particular use; what a brine is and when it would be used. They learn how to bake a cake, and how baking a cake is different from baking cookies or bars.

(3) As problem solvers, students should be able to recommend foods for a graduation party, and those foods should be different from what they would recommend for a child's birthday party or a black-tie event. Not only must students be able to identify the intended result (and the reasons for that choice), but they must also be able to work backward, identifying what ingredients they need, and work forward, understanding how to produce the dishes at the event, at the appropriate time, and organized in a beautiful display. In sum, students are creating for the clients what the clients themselves cannot see, but what they desire.

Law school is no different. Our ingredients are statutes, rules, formulas, definitions, case holdings, etc. Our knowledge is understanding how rules and case holdings, definitions and formulas, regulations and statutes fit together. It is about seeing the information in different forms through hypotheticals, or by synthesizing cases, or in crafting an essay. But in the end, what professors want students to be able to do is take the knowledge they have generated and create possible solutions for clients.

A. Creativity

1. Understanding That Students Must Become Creative

What professors expect students to do with the given law, facts, and client objectives is to produce something that is appropriate for the clients' circumstances. As each client's situation is unique, arguably each result is also novel. Professors have a working knowledge of the subject-matter area and easily can create just such a solution. But what professors are able to create is beyond what students are able to create. Students, as novices, are trying to understand the last rule or concept learned and have not yet pivoted to see what lies just beyond that rule or concept. More specifically, students are not yet ready to imagine that which they have not yet been told exists. But at some point, they must begin to combine concepts and facts and rules in a way that is a step beyond what they have been told. In sum, they must begin to learn to think creatively. If professors want students to think creatively, to understand how the subject-matter area *works*, to be able to effectively assist clients, they must intentionally create a learning environment in which students acquire this skill.

Creativity is generally thought of as something new to everyone, something that had not existed before. But there is no reason that creativity, as a component of a learning environment, should be viewed as including only those things that are unique in the world. Rather, it can include students' ability to create something unique with their own knowledge. In this way, creativity is a skill with which students produce a solution that is both novel and appropriate to the circumstances, based on their understanding of the law and the facts.

As with any skill, it must be learned and practiced. First, students must understand case holdings, statutes, regulations, and rules, and how each of those pieces interacts with the others. This information and knowledge is highly static and mostly nonmalleable, easily captured in outlines and study guides. The next step is the difficult step, the step that is dynamic and synergistic, and that cannot be extracted from an outline. To acquire the skill of creativity, students must learn to work their way to the edge of the knowledge they understand and reach forward into something that is not in the outline or class notes.

The ability to think creatively distinguishes the competent tradesmen, who are just applying rules they have learned to relatively unvarying fact patterns, from lawyers who can respond resourcefully to the specific problems and needs of clients. Unless law school graduates want merely to cut and paste documents or repeat predetermined steps, achieving mastery of the rules is not enough. They must be able to go beyond that, to synthesize concepts, create new legal tools, and imagine novel ways of solving different problems. This level of creativity is sometimes called "ideation fluency"—the ability to generate numerous alternative hypotheses applicable to each problem. In other words, it is the ability to produce a large number of responses to a problem and to continue to produce responses over a longer period of time than those who lack the skill of creativity. Part of being an effective and successful lawyer requires the lawyer to not only identify the correct result, but also to identify a number of ways to reach that result.

2. Law School Is Not Currently Designed to Help Students to Learn to Be Creative

The current law school format is not designed to promote independent thinking or risk-taking, much less creativity. For the most part, the grading system rewards students who repeat what the professor said to them and wants to hear students say back. Essay questions intentionally are written so all can be graded with a standardized rubric—every student is expected to give the same answer based on the information the professor gave. Multiple-choice questions are built around an expectation that all students should process through each question in a standardized way.

To the extent that students are confirming that they have learned the foundational information or have begun building knowledge, these approaches are serving their purpose. But it must be recognized that this type of learning does not encompass the third goal: it neither expects nor encourages students to begin to think creatively about the knowledge. Rather than answering other people's questions, a focus on creativity requires students to develop their own questions. Rather than walking through foundational knowledge as part of a mental task, a creativity-oriented environment rewards those who go beyond recitation of knowledge to see multiple novel and workable solutions to a problem.

Professor Prompts:

1. When you ask a question, do you already have an answer in mind?
   If yes, why do you ask the question?

2. Do you ask questions for which there is more than one answer or no clear answer?
   If no, why not?
   If yes, why?

Traditionally, legal education has not created spaces for creative thinking. Particularly when using the case method of learning, students are burdened with long reading assignments and are expected to extract from that reading a few basic rules or concepts. So much effort is put into extracting those rules that there is little time left in which to explore when and how those rules can be used to solve problems. This approach is starting to change. Professors are beginning to recognize that so much more can be learned when class time is used to discover the edges and flavor of the law, rather than for just teasing out more traditional black-letter rules.

Without intending to do so, sometimes a professor might discourage creative questions because of a desire to get through certain material in a class session. To that professor, certain questions may seem "off-topic" or not quite on point. Or course, it is not always possible to answer every student question in a given class. But, erring on the side of tackling questions, even those that may seem a bit off the topic to the professor, can create a classroom environment that supports creative problem-solving for students and future lawyers. Even if every question cannot be addressed, professors should encourage students to ask questions that challenge the paradigms and rules, both inside and outside of class.

Alternative Approach to Covering a Case: Rather than using the Socratic method to extract from students the holding of a case, give students the rule and require them to develop a factual scenario in which that rule would be used. Use class time to explore the variety of suggested applications. (Students could read the case after the class discussion.)

1. Did students understand the rule well enough to create factual scenarios to which it would apply?

> 2. How wide-ranging were the suggested factual scenarios?
> 3. Did some students suggest facts to which the rule applied, while other suggested facts to which it would not apply?
> 4. Did any of the suggested factual scenarios also implicate other rules? If so, did students recognize this fact?

The exam structure of a traditional law school course does not encourage creativity. In a traditional course that included only the final exam on which to base students' grades, the final exam would be the only time students believe they have to know the information. Students have little incentive to learn, understand, and be able to work with the material before that. At this point, of course, it is too late to take that additional step and deal creatively with the material; the opportunity for students to think creatively about their acquired knowledge with a professor's assistance has been lost.

Finally, competition and a threatening environment inhibit creativity. If we peek into the classroom and see a student standing, being grilled by the professor, any possibility of that student being creative has been squashed. Certainly, most students can be expected to do no more than get through the experience. Expecting them to think beyond answering the professor's questions or to see something the professor has not told them is unrealistic.

> **Professor Prompts:**
>
> 1. Do you consider the questions students ask during class as falling into one of two categories (those that move the discussion along and those that sidetrack the discussion)?
> 2. In responding to questions that move the discussion along, can you both anchor the response in the information you want to impart while also connecting the information to new possibilities raised by the question?

3. Making Creativity Part of Classroom Instruction

From the big-picture perspective, to bring creativity into the classroom, both students and professors must understand that rote memorization is not the objective; instead, it is just the first step on a journey designed to enable students to apply knowledge and engage in creative problem solving. Students' focus must be on developing the skill of devising alternative solutions for a client, given the law and the client's unique facts. From a more molecular perspective, to bring creativity into the classroom, three components must be present: domain-relevant knowledge, critical-thinking skills, and motivation.

1. *Domain-relevant knowledge.* Before students can develop creative thinking skills, they must have something to think about. Accordingly, content comes first. Moreover, content can be thought of in terms of complexity. For each content area, there are the most basic concepts, ideas, rules, etc., and that content grows in complexity as more complex ideas are layered on top. As different facts are considered, nuances are developed, exceptions are created, etc. As the complexity of the content increases, the thinking about that content needs to adapt to the increased challenge.

All too often, students believe they don't need to *really* learn the content until just before the final exam. This failure to truly learn content during the term in favor of last-minute cramming makes it impossible for students to learn to be creative, and it also inhibits long-term retention of the material.

> **Classroom Project:** Part of understanding the law is seeing connections among concepts. Rather than using class time to learn rules one case at a time, expose students to how concepts are integrated.
>
> Write a topic heading on the board. Ask students to identify related ideas. Write those ideas on branches linked to the topic heading. Add more ideas as sub-branches, creating as many levels as necessary.

2. *Critical-thinking skills.* Critical thinking has always been part of the fabric of law school education. Students are, first, expected to think intelligently about a myriad of issues. Second, they must be able to do more than just know the answer; they must know how to get to the answer and understand the implications of the journey.

Critical thinking is a higher-order thinking skill. Higher-order thinking requires students to use and manipulate information and ideas in ways that transform their meaning and implications. It is the kind of thinking needed to solve problems, formulate inferences, determine the likelihood of an outcome, and make decisions. It is the skill necessary to grapple with problems that are messy and ill-defined. It is multifaceted and requires judgment, analysis, and synthesis. It is more than memorizing or applying rules in a rote or mechanical manner.

It is the degree to which students can apply previous knowledge to new situations to solve problems, reach decisions, or evaluate outcomes. To truly develop the skill, students must be self-reflective about the thinking process they use to arrive at a conclusion and what factors impacted that outcome.

As a skill, critical thinking means that students are aware of their thinking and learning and are able to direct their thinking and learning. To engage in critical thinking, students must step outside their comfort zones. Most often, students just want to know "what the right answer is." Critical thinking, in contrast, involves the elements of uncertainty and unpredictability and is not designed to lead to "a right answer." It is worth noting that this reality might be as uncomfortable for some professors as it is for students.

Professor Prompts:

1. Do you ask questions that involve elements of uncertainty and unpredictability, questions without a "right" answer?
2. What do you expect of your students when you ask such a question?

Translating all of this into law practice, successful lawyers must be able to employ cognitive skills or strategies to combine the facts that clients bring with the law that lawyers know; they must identify probable outcomes for the clients, they must identify which outcomes are most likely and which are most desirable, and they must decide whether they can find any way to increase the probability of reaching the desired outcome. Lawyers who have the ability to think critically will be able to create more favorable outcomes for their clients than lawyers who have not developed, or not as fully developed, the skill of critical thinking.

Alternative Approach to Covering a Case: Rather than using the Socratic method to extract from students the holding of a case, give students the facts of the case as a client would have presented them to an attorney. Require students to propose one solution, identify one obstacle to that solution, and explain why this solution is the best path forward, even in light of that obstacle. (Students could read the case after the class discussion.)

1. Did students understand the client's problem?
2. How wide-ranging were the proposed solutions?
3. Could students anticipate any problems with their proposed solutions?
4. Did students understand their solutions well enough to be able to explain them?

3. *Motivation.* We have all sat in a class, jotting down notes, waiting for the time to pass, waiting for the class to end. The material being covered does not spark our curiosity, does not make us wonder about the next thing, does not make us question the piece of the puzzle the professor has not mentioned. We are content to follow along as the professor puts together the edge pieces of the jigsaw puzzle for us, perhaps never wondering about those center pieces or what the big picture looks like. Just as surely, we have all sat in a class where questions arrive fully formed in our heads as we stretch our knowledge toward what we cannot yet see, our minds straining to understand what it would look like if the information was turned just slightly. We likely raised our hand and asked a few questions, looked more thoroughly at the course materials, and thought about the information long after we left the classroom.

Now, standing on the other side of the podium, we want our students to be experiencing our classes under the second scenario, with a sense of wonder and curiosity. We want them to be engaged in the material, first, for the sake of appreciating a subject-matter area and, second, because a student who is engaged in the learning process has a greater depth of processing, memory, knowledge acquisition, attention, and comprehension. Engaged students generally are motivated students. In turn, motivation influences how students approach education.

Professor Prompts:

1. How motivated are your students to learn the material you are teaching?
2. How do you know?
3. Can you present the material in a manner that makes them more curious?

Alternative Approach to Covering a Case: An appellate opinion explains what transpired up to the point when the case was submitted to the court for decision. However, the lives of the parties continued after that. Rather than approaching a case using IRAC, have students consider what happened after the opinion was issued.

- What was the impact on both parties?
- Were both parties likely satisfied with the opinion?
- Would there be any impact on the parties going forward?
- Would any additional legal issues arise even though the opinion resolved the issues before the court?
- Might the parties wish they had settled the case?
- Is there an obvious basis on which they could have settled? If so, what are possible ideas about why they didn't settle?

Motivation is a continuum, with extrinsic motivation at one end of the continuum and intrinsic motivation at the other end. Extrinsic motivation is the motivation to achieve an external reward or avoid a punishment. When we are driven to reach a financial milestone or reap a reward, or we attempt to do our best because of a past or expected future evaluation, we are driven by extrinsic motivation. Intrinsic motivation comes from the inherent satisfaction of doing an activity. It is the motivation that arises from our innate interest in an activity or the simple joy of meeting a challenge found within a given task or project.

Intrinsic motivation is more successful than extrinsic motivation in promoting learning and achievement. When intrinsically motivated, people are motivated simply to perform an activity and to have the spontaneous experiences of interest, enjoyment, excitement, and satisfaction that accompany the behavior. Being driven from within allows us to explore an area with autonomy. In fact, when a person expects a reward, intrinsic motivation is undermined. This means that intimidation, deadlines, orders, and competition diminish intrinsic motivation because such things focus attention on the extrinsic reasons for doing something, thereby minimizing the importance of the original drive. But a reward for a creative accomplishment can increase intrinsic motivation.

Those who engage in a task for reasons such as interest, developing a mastery of the area, meeting a personal challenge—having an intrinsic goal orientation—engage in deeper processing. Those who engage in a task to demonstrate to others mastery, or get a good grade, or get a better grade than others—having an extrinsic goal orientation—have shallower levels of information processing.

> **Assessment Suggestion:** Provide a fact pattern presenting a client's problem. Have students create a solution to the problem and an elevator pitch* advocating for this solution.
>
> 1. Did students understand the problem?
> 2. Would the proposed solution resolve the problem?
> 3. Does the elevator pitch adequately and appropriately represent the problem and solution?
>
> * An elevator pitch is a short speech (no longer than the length of an elevator ride) that a listener can readily and easily understand.

Current law school environment. Even though research shows that students who will learn best are those who are intrinsically motivated, our current education system, law school in particular, works *against* learning deriving from a place of intrinsic motivation. Each student's level of learning is captured in a grade and from there in a grade point average (GPA), which really reflects the extent to which a student has learned what the professor deemed important enough to put on the exam; the grade may have no reflection on the student's level of engagement with the material or the extent to which the student deeply learned the material. The grading system is an extrinsic-based reward system, and it is one that has been shown to decrease creativity.

A student's grade and GPA, the extrinsically focused measures of the student's ability or aptitude, then become a springboard for the student's success, perhaps playing a role in whether he gets accepted on law review, gets an interview, or gets the summer internship position. Because of the role it can play in his future, the student must focus on his GPA, even as he recognizes that it might not have captured the amount of learning, understanding, or effort he put into the class. Moreover, it is possible that his GPA does not reflect his desire to learn, ability to learn, or aptitude to solve problems. In sum, it is unlikely that a GPA reflects the student's level of intrinsic motivation.

This failure to reward intrinsic motivation is particularly troubling in that intrinsic motivation leads students to think more creatively, to become better problem solvers and be able to represent clients with understanding and common sense. It ignores the fact that recognizing and appreciating creative ideas and providing constructive feedback to students trying to develop the skill of creativity works to create the graduates we want—those who can create something beyond what they heard in the classroom.

Professor Prompts:

1. Is your classroom structured to reward students who are extrinsically motived or intrinsically motivated?
2. What steps could you take to reward students who are intrinsically motivated?

B. Assessment Suggestions

Critical thinking skills. For developing critical thinking skills, the structure of the class is perhaps less important than the behaviors that occur in the classroom. At a minimum, what happens in the classroom can help persuade students that basic information and knowledge acquisition should happen during the term and not at the end of the term. Specifically, students who will be called upon to use information and knowledge, and use it as part of higher-order thinking and in a meaningful way, are much more motivated to learn than students who know that they will not be expected to have acquired that information or knowledge until the final exam.

In deciding whether classroom instruction should be altered, it is important to realize that when professors alter how they interact with students, the outcome of the instruction necessarily will vary. The focus should be on creating an environment of active student involvement that fairly and consistently challenges the students' higher-order thinking skills.

Professor Prompts:

1. In what ways do you interact with your students?
2. In what ways do these interactions promote higher-order thinking skills, in particular critical thinking skills?
3. How many students are demonstrating critical thinking skills during each class?
4. What is the ratio of the time that students talk to the time that you talk?
5. In what ways can you increase student involvement in the class?
6. In what ways can you increase the number of students demonstrating critical thinking skills?
7. In what ways can you increase the level at which students are expected to think critically?
8. Can you challenge students' understanding of the material in a way that is fair and works to develop their understanding of the material?
9. What type of feedback do you give students?
10. Are you intentional in your feedback, structuring it so that it will help students to refine their higher-order thinking skills?

Assessment Suggestions: Critical thinking is perhaps the most important skill students could learn. Help each student test this ability. With an eye to the following questions, provide students with a client-based fact pattern and have them answer the following three questions:

1. What legal problem do you see?
2. What three facts alerted you that the identified legal problem exists?
3. What additional piece of information do you need to resolve the client's problem?

Motivation. The classroom should be an environment that bolsters students' intrinsic motivation. The professor should seek to confirm students' competence or enable them to become more deeply involved in work that they are becoming excited about. By enhancing intrinsic motivation, creativity can also be enhanced.

Professor Prompts:

1. In what ways can you connect the subject matter of your class to the areas of practice that your students intend to engage in?
2. In how many ways can you connect the subject matter of your class to the everyday life of a practicing attorney?
3. In how many ways can you connect the subject matter of your class to the everyday life of a law graduate who is not practicing law?

The bottom line. Professors want students to leave class with the ability to use what they have learned to help clients solve problems. In other words, professors want students to understand how the subject-matter area works, so that they can create novel, client-centered solutions based on unique sets of facts.

The skill of creativity doesn't automatically arrive when students acquire knowledge of the subject matter. Just like every other skill, students must develop it themselves. Professors can assist students in this development by creating a class where students are held accountable throughout the entire term for acquiring the necessary knowledge, where critical thinking is part of the fabric of every class, and where students are motivated to try harder each class period. Through this triad, professors create an environment where students can begin to see what lies just beyond the rule or concept the professor has told them exists. By developing the skill of creativity, students will develop the ability to create something unique with respect to their own knowledge, something that is novel and appropriate to the circumstances, and something that will address the clients' issues.

Alternative Approach to Covering a Case: Rather than approaching a case using IRAC, do not assign the court's opinion as part of the reading assignment. Rather, provide students with the facts of a case as if presented by the client during an intake interview. If possible, find the facts as presented to the lower court in the briefs.

1. Ask students to identify the problem from the client's perspective.
2. Ask students to identify the problem from the lawyer's perspective.
3. Ask students to explain why the client and lawyer see the problem differently.
4. In class, take five minutes to brainstorm solutions to problems.
5. Identify which solutions address the problem from the client's perspective, from the lawyer's perspective, and from both perspectives.

Chapter 8 Workbook

Creating New Outcomes: Working toward Creativity

I. Background

Course: _____

Professors want students to be able to understand how the subject-matter area *works*, to understand how the knowledge can be used to benefit a client. In other words, students must be able to *do*, not just *know*. This "doing" is not simply responding to hypotheticals that professors use to expound on the material covered during a class. This "doing" is what happens when students begin the practice of law.

Complete the following chart to make a connection between what practitioners do and how students' learning will ready them for that activity.

Connecting the Classroom to the Practice of Law:

What practitioners do:	Classroom activities/instruction:

In deciding whether classroom instruction should be altered, it is important to realize that when you change how you interact with your students, the outcome of your instruction necessarily will also change. The focus should be on creating an environment of active student involvement that fairly and consistently challenges students' higher-order thinking skills.

Answer the following questions:

	Question	Answer
1.	In what ways do I interact with my students?	
2.	In what ways do my interactions promote higher-order thinking skills, in particular critical thinking skills?	
3.	How many students are demonstrating critical thinking skills during each class?	
4.	What is the ratio of the time that students talk to the time that I talk?	
5.	In what ways can I increase student involvement in the class?	
6.	In what ways can I increase the number of students demonstrating critical thinking skills?	
7.	In what ways can I increase the level at which students are expected to think critically?	
8.	Can I challenge students' understanding of the material in a way that is fair and works to develop their understanding of the material?	
9.	What type of feedback do I give students?	
10.	Am I intentional in my feedback, structuring it so that it will help students to refine their higher-order thinking skills?	

Part of understanding the law is seeing connections among concepts. Use the following steps to create your own mind map. Please keep in mind that the objective of a mind map is to show *connections* between concepts. It is *not* intended to be hierarchal, like an outline.

Mind Map:

1.	Select a topic. Write it in the middle of a blank piece of paper.
2.	Identify related ideas and connect them to the topic through branches.
3.	Add sub-branches, creating as many levels and connections as necessary.

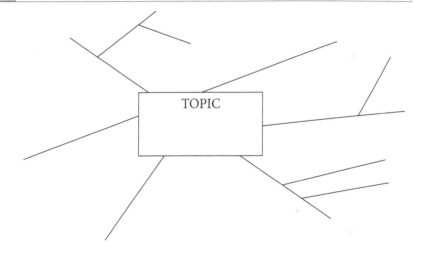

Question: After having seen connections among topics, do you think about the content area differently?	Answer:

Those who engage in a task for reasons such as interest, developing a mastery of the area, meeting a personal challenge — an intrinsic goal orientation — engage in deeper processing. Those who engage in a task to demonstrate to others mastery, or get a good grade, or get a better grade than others — an extrinsic goal orientation — have shallower levels of information processing.

Identify the ways in which you motivate your students, considering both intrinsic and extrinsic motivation.

Intrinsic	Extrinsic
1.	1.
2.	2.
3.	3.
4.	4.
5.	5.

Are there ways that you can make your students more curious about the subject matter? What are they?

Increasing Curiosity
1.
2.
3.
4.

II. Each Class Period

A worksheet should be completed for each class period and each major topic covered in that class period.

Class Period: _____

Topics to Be Covered:

1. _____

2. _____

3. _____

For each topic, create one question for which you have an expected answer and one question for which you do not have an expected answer:

Question with expected answer:	Question for which there is not an expected answer:

For the question listed above, explain why you would ask it:

Reason for the question with expected answer:	Reason for question for which there is not an expected answer:

When students learn law by reading cases, they start with the outcome and move backward. They are shown which facts were important, what law applied, and how the answer was arrived at. All the difficult thinking has been done for them.

Practitioners start with the facts and move forward. Starting with only the facts and moving forward is much more difficult. The practitioner must possess subject-matter area knowledge, engage in critical thinking, and create solutions. To really help students understand the skills needed to be effective lawyers, the professor must make a shift from the thinking being done for students to students doing the thinking:

1.	How can you present the course content so that students are challenged to begin with facts and move forward, thinking critically, demonstrating subject-matter area knowledge, and offering solutions?	
2.	How can you use a court's opinion to not only move backward into the facts, law, and analysis, but to move forward in a way that requires students to think independently?	

Chapter 9

Enhancing the Classroom Environment for Students Who Have Learning Disabilities (Without Taking Anything Away from Those Who Do Not)

It is almost certain that every entering law school class contains students with disabilities. Some might have physical disabilities; others might have psychological disabilities. But a number are likely to have learning disabilities or other learning problems. Sometimes students have been diagnosed before they arrive at law school. But more often, they have not.

One would expect that students would be tested for learning disabilities while still young and that most learning disabilities would be diagnosed timely. Both expectations would be wrong. Many, many students in post-graduate education have undiagnosed learning disabilities. One reason that students are not diagnosed is that schools are disincentivized from referring students for testing. After all, if students get diagnosed with learning disabilities, then the school has to provide services: individualized education programs, special education programs, extra resources, and extra support. All of this costs money, and schools don't have enough money as it is. Thus, unless a student is a behavior problem, the school may have no incentive to have the student tested. Furthermore, some students never get tested because of cultural barriers: some sub-parts of the population simply do not believe in getting this type of testing, either because of past discrimination or because the beliefs and practices of a particular culture make it taboo.

One might also expect that students who have undiagnosed learning disabilities will not make it into post-graduate education such as law school. Again, that would be wrong. Humans are persistent and ingenious, and people with learning difficulties find a way. They develop coping strategies that allow them to do what they have to; they change their college majors to avoid having to do things that are difficult for them, and they seek outside resources and other kinds of supports. They find a way. So though some testing professionals believe that there cannot be disabled people in post-graduate education, they are wrong.

Screening for Learning Problems:

At every first-year orientation, administer the Nelson-Denny Reading Test as a screening device for reading fluency problems. The reading test has two components: vocabulary and comprehension. The scores are standardized—that is, the results are reported as percentiles that compare this student's performance with others at the same education level. The students' scores can be standardized against second-term college seniors (because that is the highest grade level available for the test). All students who score at the 25th percentile in one or both parts of the test receive an email suggesting that they may want to go for educational testing to check for learning problems. Students who are diagnosed with learning problems may qualify for accommodations such as extra time on exams, a private room, spacing the exams out so that they are not back-to-back, access to a program that reads text aloud to the student, the use of formula sheets, etc.

When a person goes for educational testing, the testing professional generally administers a whole battery of tests in an effort to measure as many different brain functions as possible. Thinking, reading, learning, attention, and problem solving involve many different steps and many different types of thinking. Every brain function is potentially on a bell curve. A person's ability to perform any particular function can range from very low to very high. And every person will have a unique constellation of strengths and weaknesses. If an individual has high potential but performs at a lower level than would be expected or has less achievement than would be expected, the testing professional looks for patterns in the highs and lows to diagnose a particular learning disability. The otherwise unexplainable gap between what the person's potential would tell us to expect and the person's actual performance is what we call a learning disability. Or the pattern in the lows and highs may cause a person to be diagnosed with attention problems, an anxiety disorder, obsessive-compulsive tendencies, etc.

More people have learning disabilities or other learning problems than any of us would have expected. As time goes on and we learn more about the brain and about learning, it seems likely that it will appear to become still more common. The more we know about thinking, the more we will learn about variations and abnormalities.

Another thing to keep in mind: students with learning disabilities or learning problems are usually either of normal intelligence or they are above average. Again, disabilities manifest themselves because of the gap between expected performance and actual performance. A person with low intelligence is less likely to have a gap that is statistically significant because that person's expected performance will be low anyway.

The point is that you are very likely to have students with diagnosed or undiagnosed learning difficulties in your classroom. Furthermore, those students are likely very bright. The question is this: what can you do to enhance their learning experiences, help level the playing field for them, and to help them achieve their potential? What follows is a list of strategies that you can use that will increase your chances of helping your students. And the good news is that every single strategy will benefit the non-challenged students as well.

A. The Problem: Slow Processing Speed

One of the problems that many students suffer from is slow processing speed. That means that when the student is being presented with information, whether visually or auditorily, their brains process that information a little bit more slowly than people who do not process slowly. This has a number of very damaging effects. First, it makes reading much more difficult. The brain has only a few "slots" in short-term memory, and those slots hold information for only a short time. When a person reads quickly, the brain pulls meaning from the words in a sentence, then combines the words to create meaning, then stores that meaning. Then the brain goes on to the next sentence and does the same thing. At the end of the paragraph, the brain takes the bits from the sentences and turns them into meaning over the whole paragraph. And as the reader goes from paragraph to paragraph, the reader accumulates the meaning over the entire passage. The reader is interpreting text, storing the meaning, combining meaning, and storing that meaning, then getting more, all very quickly.

But when a person reads slowly, the pieces of information the reader just stored evaporate before the next pieces can be brought into memory. The person may fail to recognize words or miss words or mentally add words that aren't there. And when slow processors try to read more quickly than their brains can go, they get nothing from what they read. The effect is that the reader must re-read, over and over, until enough can be stored and processed so that the meaning of the passage can finally come through. (If you see students who process text slowly, you can suggest that the student try a coping mechanism such as annotating the text. The student can write notes to the side of the text that summarize what each piece of text said. This makes the page a substitute for memory. The reader can read just the annotations, which can make it easier to collect the ideas and see the big-picture flow of the ideas. Another aid is to use a computer that reads text out loud.)

Similarly, slow processing has a dramatic effect on a person's ability to benefit from listening because they cannot listen fast enough. Most speakers go from "old" information to "new" information. They begin with the information that was previously introduced and then move to the new part, the point of today's lesson. When a person with normal processing speed is listening, that person will very quickly process that old information and then be ready to receive the new information, which the person will then process quickly enough to keep up with the flow. However, when a person who processes slowly is listening, that person will be "stuck" on the old information for much longer. This means that when the teacher has moved on to the new information, the student is still on the old information. As the teacher moves through the different stages of the new information, the student cannot keep up with the flow. The student usually picks up on some of the pieces but misses others.

Solution: Slow Down

One way to help is to slow down. Don't try to talk quickly. Don't get excited and get away from the students. Give them time to process all the parts. Slow down.

Another way to help is to make recordings. You can do this two ways. First, flip your classroom and make recordings (preferably video recordings) of you going through the information. Make these recordings available at least one day before class so that students can become familiar with it before class begins. That way, they may be able to "listen faster." Second, if you use slides or other visual aids during class, make them available at least a day before class. That gives the students time to read and process the slides before class begins. Third, record your actual class and make that available to your students. Let students know that you will be recording, and encourage them to monitor their own listening. If the student realizes that she lost the flow at a particular point during class, have her write down the time. Then the student can go to the parts of the recording where the problems occurred without having to re-listen to the whole class. By the way, a number of your students are likely to listen to the whole class recording and re-take notes. For a student who processes very slowly or who has attention problems, that can be a lifesaver—it is likely to be the student's only real opportunity to take good notes.

And your non-slow-processing students will benefit, too.

B. The Problem: Not Seeing Relationships Within Information

Information in law school is complex and detailed, and students must see the relationships among concepts and see how information is organized within concepts. To learn and to use the law, students must identify the major topics and what will trigger them. Then, they must see what sub-parts make up each major topic. Then, they must see what sub-topics make up each sub-part. Finally, they must see what elements, steps, or rules each sub-topic contains. (This is the reason that we tell students to write outlines.) Furthermore, the information in text or in lectures may be structured in many different ways: chronologically (like the concepts in Civil Procedure: the topics can be arranged into a timeline, which runs from before the filing of the complaint, through discovery and summary judgment, through trial and appeal); main idea/detail (like the elements of crimes and what each element requires); comparison/contrast; cause and effect; or problem/solution. Some students have profound difficulty in seeing those structures in information—they may simply see all information as lists of bullet points, as linear text without hierarchy or connections.

Solution: Help Students Map the Material

Teach students how you find the structure inside information. One way is to ask them to look at major concepts first and think about how they relate to each other. Then, look at each major concept and ask what the subparts are and how they relate. Then, look at each subpart and ask what is inside of it.

The top level is like being in a plane at 60,000 feet, looking down at the ground. You can see major geographical features—a lake, a city, a river, a mountain, and where they are in relation to each other—but you cannot see details. If you then focus on one of those item and zoom down to 20,000 feet, you will see the prominent features of that item, but again, no details. If you then zoom down to 5,000 feet, you will see all the characteristics of the prominent features. And then if you zoom down to ground level, you will see the details. This is a visual description of the process of chunking—going from the highest level, through successively lower levels, until you reach the lowest level where the details live. You are not *supposed* to see the details at the highest level—only at the lowest level.

You could do this with your students with various legal concepts and teach them how you do it. If you are working with, for example, Secured Transactions, start with the UCC and the table of contents. Show them how you look only at the major headings, how you think about their relationship to each other, and how you come up with the big-picture steps in a Secured Transaction analysis (60,000 feet). Then go to a chapter and talk about how you figure out where it goes in the big picture; then look at how the sub-headings relate to each other. Is the first rule the general, generic rule and the rest of the rules fact driven? Do the rules form a sequence that the law requires you to follow (20,000 feet)? Then go to a particular rule and show students how you map that rule. Again, what are the major parts of the rule? How do they connect to each other? When would you need to use them (5,000 feet)? Then go to the details of the individual paragraphs of the rule. Teach students how you break the text up into individual details that make up the analysis. Show them how to figure out what facts would or would not satisfy the requirements. Then have students do the same process with other law.

Make the maps as visual as you can. Think about using things like color coding. Use symbols that represent abstract concepts as a means to help students create memory aids. Use spatial relationships and white space on paper to help you demonstrate connections or lack of connections among ideas. Change font size, using larger font for major concepts, smaller for sub-concepts, and the smallest for the details. Suggest that your students use easel paper, freezer paper, or melamine sheets to cover a wall and turn the wall into the outline.

C. The Problem: Lack of Focus

Everybody's mind wanders sometimes. But some students have a much bigger problem with staying focused, either because of Attention Deficit Disorder

(ADD) or Attention Deficit Hyperactivity Disorder (ADHD) or because of anxiety problems.

Possible Solution: Build Relationships

When students have a relationship with you, staying focused is a little bit easier because they care about you, and they know that you care about them. Generally, students want to focus—they do not want to drift. Emotional connections with you give an extra push that might help students to stay more focused.

Possible Solution: Vary Activities

Don't do the same thing all the way through class. Give students the chance to do different things. Have them work on a problem together. Then, have them explain how to solve it. Then, have other students critique the first group's work. Lecture for a few minutes, then give them a multiple-choice question to solve. Have them discuss why the wrong answers are wrong. Have individuals or groups work on outlining a concept and then present their outlines. Change the activities frequently.

As part of this, remember to make students do the work. Let them do a lot of the talking. Have them teach the material. Make sure that they are involved. A student who is actively engaged is probably focused.

Possible Solution: Make It Visual

This won't solve the problem, but it can ameliorate its effects. As you are explaining anything to students, make a visual record. Whether you are in the classroom or doing a one-on-one appointment with a student, always have a pen and pad of paper, or use a document camera, or have a board to write on, or have a slide for students to look at. Making a visual record is *essential* for students with attention problems. ADD comes in different flavors. Some students have hyperactivity; some do not. But one characteristic that ADD always features is that the student's mind is like a TV remote control. The student's mind will be on the "important" thing, on you and the thing that you are trying to teach, but then the channel changes, and the student's mind is on something else. That something else leads to another something else, and from there the student's mind goes to yet another thing. Eventually the remote comes all the way back around, and the student is with you again. But not for long. Within a very short time, the student is "gone" again. And every time the student "comes back," she has to reconstruct what has happened during the time she was gone. If you create a visual record of the flow of the lesson, the student has more clues to help with the reconstruction. The student will be able to look at the notes that you took and backfill what happened while the student was drifting.

D. The Problem: Lack of Memory Building

Some students are naïve about building memory. Many students think that it should be natural or easy to memorize things, and they may despair when they have trouble. Many students think that rote memory is the right way to build memory. For example, they may think that reading their outlines over and over will work. Or they think that writing them out over and over again is a productive strategy. But, of course, the latter is an extremely time- and labor-intensive means. It would be great to get the same result with less time and work. Furthermore, rote memory is not the type of deep, stable memory that students need to be able to access under stressful exam conditions.

The Solution: Teach Strategies for Building Memory

Using multiple strategies together will be more likely to produce long-lasting memory. For example, building memory palaces will help students to keep big-picture flow in mind. To build a memory palace, a person must see the big items that make up a concept or a process. Each process is assigned a symbol that stands for the essence of that part, and the symbol should be something that is memorable to the user. Then the user creates some sort of story involving the symbols to make the symbols memorable. By remembering the story, the user remembers the symbols; the symbols then remind the user of the details of each part.

Related to this is the idea of thinking about how or why things work. Rather than trying to memorize the details, think about the logic of how it works. Deep understanding replaces rote memory. For example, using old exam questions and planning out the answers to them enables students to see how certain facts make certain legal things happen. Humans are naturally drawn to stories—stories are memorable to people. So to remember the law, students can try to remember the facts. The facts elicit the law that corresponds to those facts. Once a student has practiced with several exam questions representing a concept, the student is more likely to be able to reproduce the analysis for that concept.

Another strategy is spaced repetition. When a person learns something, the brain starts to forget almost immediately. But actively refreshing the information in memory slows down the rate of forgetting. The more times the person refreshes the information, the more slowly the information will be forgotten, which is why spaced repetition is vital for learning large amounts of information that the person wants to retain indefinitely—like, for example, learning law for a bar exam. A strategy for doing this might be to use the headings in an outline as prompts, then recite what the student knows about the prompt, and then check the outline to see what the student did not know. Then store the information again, and recite it from memory again. The student should also use some sort of visual marker to keep track of how many times the student has touched the material. A standard method is to put a red mark next to information that is not yet in memory. Once the student can consistently recall the information, the student should mark it in green. And the marks will be a visual reminder of how many times the student has touched that material.

Another Solution: Touch as Many Parts of the Brain as Possible

Different parts of the brain perform different functions and solve different problems in different ways. If people have difficulty in processing information in one way, then giving them the same information in various ways that touch different parts of the brain can give them the opportunity to use more than one problem-solving approach on the same problem. If you make lessons as multisensory as possible, then you can help students with a deficiency in one area to draw on other areas that might be stronger, or maybe just different. That means that it is not enough to talk about an idea; instead, draw it out. Set it to music. Turn it into a story that symbolizes the important steps, and create a voice-over narrative explaining what is happening at each step. Act it out.

All of these techniques will help your students who have learning problems. And the good news is that they will all work even better for students who do not have learning problems.

Conclusion

Law school has been taught primarily using the case method approach for so long, sometimes it is difficult to imagine it any other way. And maybe more importantly, it is difficult for professors to understand why it might need to be any different. Professors learned the law that way, so students can learn that way as well.

The current approach to teaching law school ignores the fact that the practice of law involves much more than the ability to read appellate cases. An attorney must be able to figure out the client's goals, negotiate a solution, be aware of statutes of limitations, identify evidentiary issues, realize when ethical issues arise, etc. The current approach to teaching, with content being delivered in silos, does not address this reality.

Moreover, is there a more compelling reason to change instructional approach than that students will learn more? Active learning techniques and assessments are different ways to teach the same material. Education research tells us that these techniques improve student learning. Furthermore, they build the skills students need to practice law and continue learning when they leave the classroom.

Most professors believe that, because they need to cover the requisite cases, they don't have any time to assist their students in developing skills. But if the focus remains on content coverage, what is missing is any focus on what students are actually learning. In the end, if students do not understand and cannot meaningfully use the information being presented by the professor, has any learning really happened?

The change in educational approach can happen slowly. Each term, professors could select and complete one or two worksheets to refocus the instructional design of the course. They could also consider adding one skills-based exercise into the doctrinal course. In a short time, they will have built a stronger, more robust course. These chapters offer many suggestions for skills-based approaches that could be used in any course. Note that these approaches are simply a different method of covering the material and cases, but this method shifts the focus from what students have read to what they understand.

In a short time, professors will have a workable mixture of both instruction and checking in with students about what they have learned. They will have made the shift in approach from "Did I teach X?" to "Did they learn X?" and students will have learned more and be better prepared for the practice of law.

Index